# *driven*

## beyond the call of God

# *driven*

## beyond the call of God

### discovering the rhythms of grace

# PAMELA EVANS

Published by
**The Bible Reading Fellowship**
Peter's Way, Sandy Lane West
Oxford OX4 5HG
ISBN 1 84101 054 5

First published 1999
10 9 8 7 6 5 4 3 2 1 0

**Acknowledgments**
Unless otherwise stated, scripture quotations are taken from the Holy Bible, *New International
Version*, copyright © 1973, 1978, 1984 by the International Bible Society. Published by Hodder &
Stoughton. Used by permission.
Scripture taken from *The Message*. Copyright © by Eugene H. Peterson, 1993, 1994, 1995. Used
by permission of Navpress Publishing Group.
Scripture taken from *The New Testament in Modern English*. Copyright © by J.B. Phillips, 1960.
Used by permission of HarperCollins Publishers.
The song *I am a wounded soldier*, by Danny Daniels. Copyright © 1985 Mercy/Vineyard
Publishing/Music Services, administered by CopyCare, P.O. Box 77, Hailsham, BN27 3EF, UK.
Used by permission.
Extract from Eddie Askew's book *Cross Purposes*. Copyright © 1995 The Leprosy Mission
International, 80 Windmill Road, Brentford, Middlesex TW8 0QH, UK. Used by permission.
Extracts from *Twelve Steps*: copyright material (AAWS) reprinted with permission.

A catalogue record for this book
is available from the British Library

Printed and bound in Great Britain by
Caledonian Book Manufacturing International, Glasgow

# Contents

# Acknowledgments

It would be impossible to acknowledge every person who has contributed to this book. During its long gestation many things which I saw and heard sparked my thinking, sometimes unbeknown to those involved. Stories of personal battles and suffering touched me very deeply and spurred me on. Some of these are told in the book, but the majority are not, because this would have necessitated a betrayal of trust. To those courageous friends who have given permission for me to retell their stories I am greatly indebted. Gail's story, with which the book begins, is fictional, but all the others are taken from the lives of real people. In most instances, names and details have been changed to prevent identification. The story which is described as coming from a counselling situation is a composite of several clients.

Those I am delighted to be able to acknowledge by name include the four dear friends who make up my support group: Shirley Green, Mary Key, Rosemary Kirk and Barbara Wood. They agreed to walk alongside me, supporting me and praying for me, while I wrote the book and brought it to publication. They have loved me enough to listen, to challenge, to encourage, to listen even more. They helped me to stay focused when I began to fear that nothing would come of all this writing. Lin Button has been the best sort of friend for over twenty years, and has enriched my spiritual journey more than any other human being. Molly Dow made perceptive and fruitful criticisms of an early draft of the book. The Revd Chris Key, the rector of the church I attend, has helped in many ways, not least by demonstrating a transparency that others have assured me is not possible for those in church leadership. Chris has also encouraged me to be 'me', and to use my gifts, as did the previous rector, the Revd John Greed. I am grateful that many members of St Helen's parish have supported me with prayer and encouragement; those who tried out the studies at the end of the book prior to the final draft made numerous helpful suggestions.

A special word of thanks is due to the Revd Paul Dunthorne for providing answers to my queries about New Testament Greek. He also acted as a sounding-board while I tried to think through a variety of issues in the light of scripture. Responsibility for any errors or inaccuracies contained in the book does, of course, lie with me.

Pamela Evans

# Counselling

The word 'counselling' is used in this book to mean the provision of a confidential relationship within which a person can safely express troublesome thoughts and feelings, and marshall the resources to move towards acceptance and/or such personal change as they choose to initiate.

# Gail's story

Gail heard the sound of her husband's key in the door just as she had finally settled Tom for the night. She crept down the stairs quietly, hoping that the noise of his arrival wouldn't unsettle Tom, or his baby sister Joanna.

'Sorry I'm late, darling,' said Richard.

'I'll get your dinner out of the oven,' said Gail.

'I'm not sure there's time to eat,' said Richard. 'I was due at Anne's ten minutes ago for that meeting about the church hall repairs, and I promised Fred I'd return his book, so I'd better drop that in on the way. I haven't had time to read it yet, but he wants to lend it to someone else…'

'But you must eat *something*,' said Gail. 'I'll do a sandwich for you to take with you.'

Richard disappeared upstairs and returned clutching a bulging file of papers, some of which escaped to the floor as he reached out for the sandwich.

'I hope I shan't be too late,' he said, shepherding his errant papers back into the file. He picked up Fred's book from the hall table, brushed a passing kiss on Gail's cheek, dived out of the door and into the car. Gail watched as he reversed out of the drive and drove off, taking a bite of the sandwich.

Gail closed the door quietly, and went into the dining-room. Collecting piled music books from the top of the piano, she transferred them to the table and sat down. The music which had been chosen to go with next month's sermon series included several new songs, and Gail wanted to sing them through to herself before trying to teach them to others.

The phone rang. Gail jumped to get it before it woke the children. It was Simon.

'Gail, Fran asked me to ring you. She's had an urgent call to visit someone she prayed for last week. By the time she gets back it'll be too late to prepare the Bible study for tomorrow morning, and she wondered if you could do it for her.'

Gail's thoughts went to the large pile of music on the dining-room table, and she hesitated.

'I know you're busy,' said Simon, 'but I've already tried Sue and Connie, and they're both out at the meeting at Anne's. I'm not sure what to do if you can't take it on.'

Gail decided the music would have to wait. She was just clearing it away and reaching for her Bible when she remembered that she'd promised to deliver a casserole to the Watsons tomorrow. Gill Watson was in hospital for an operation, and her husband Ted was holding the fort at home while trying to keep the church office ticking over. Gail carried her Bible into the kitchen and opened the freezer, trying to remember whether or not it contained anything suitable.

The phone rang again. Gail did her best to close the freezer door before rushing off to answer it. Reg's voice boomed down the line.

'Out again, is he? Well, I must speak to him—it's really urgent. Please get him to phone me when he gets back—I don't mind how late it is.'

'But I *do* mind,' thought Gail wearily, as she returned to the kitchen to continue her search of the freezer. She wondered if Reg needed any sleep at all. He certainly didn't behave as if he thought anyone else did! The meetings he held for house group leaders never finished much before midnight, and last weekend he'd phoned at eight o'clock on Saturday morning to pick Richard's brains about something. Richard had told him that he wasn't sure he *had* any brains at that time on a Saturday morning. Reg hadn't seemed to take the point.

Having successfully located four chicken pieces and put them to defrost overnight, Gail put the kettle on. She reached for her Bible again, and prayed that the Lord's inspiration would penetrate through a developing headache.

The phone rang again. It was the senior pastor, Jack. Could Richard phone him when he got in? He wanted to tell him about the extra leadership meeting arranged for breakfast-time on Saturday morning. That was the only time when no one had prior commitments. Gail sighed and reached for the paracetamol.

*Are you tired? Worn out? Burned out on religion? Come to me. Get away with me and you'll recover your life. I'll show you how to take a real rest. Walk with me and work with me— watch how I do it. Learn the unforced rhythms of grace. I won't lay anything heavy or ill-fitting on you. Keep company with me and you'll learn to live freely and lightly.*

Matthew 11:28–30, *The Message*

# Introduction: Religion can damage your health

## Luke 10:27

*'Love the Lord your God with all your heart and with all your*
*soul and with all your strength and with all your mind'; and,*
*'Love your neighbour as yourself.'*

In attempting to serve the church and our neighbour with all our
hearts and minds and strength, we can find ourselves sucked into
a lifestyle which undermines our very purpose and makes non-
sense of our message.

It's all too easy to work the treadmill called 'church' until we're
worn out, and alienated from our families. To them we may have
become the tired and irritable strangers who are never at home to
take their own incessant phone calls. This is particularly the case
if we belong to a fellowship in which all the important people,
upon whom others model their style of discipleship, are perenni-
ally exhausted. Some give the impression that they see time off as
a cop-out for spiritual failures or evidence of lack of commitment.
Even going out to work can be seen as a 'necessary evil', interrupting as it does the 'real work' which God has ordained!

Much that passes for Christian fervour is workaholism with a
religious gloss. Workaholism doesn't just affect people in their
place of work. Leisure activities, worship and Christian service
can also be affected by drivenness. A leader can set a workaholic
pace for a house group, or even for a whole fellowship. This inevitably affects the discipleship style of the members, not to mention their health, marriages, and families, and perhaps also their
performance at work.

So why do we do it? Why do we rush around attempting the
impossible on a daily basis? If we can see that our diary would

need ten-day weeks with forty-eight-hour days to accommodate all our commitments, why don't we admit that it doesn't make sense? Have friends given up trying to include us in their plans because we're always at the soup kitchen (or the counselling centre, or the drop-in club)? If so, are we relieved that they've stopped insisting that we need a night off? Or do we have a sneaking feeling that something is wrong somewhere?

If family relationships have been reduced to fleeting exchanges on the doorstep and notes on the hall table, perhaps supplemented by a weekly row over Sunday lunch, it's probably easier to keep on keeping on, than to pause and question what is happening. If we're sustaining a high-pace church-based lifestyle which includes much concern for those in need, the temptation can be to blame the resulting stress, failing health, shoddy marriage and disillusioned children on the Evil One—and battle on.

Part of the problem may be that our view of what God requires of us has congealed out of our worst fears (such as: 'God is a perfectionist slave-driver who takes delight in setting impossible tasks') rather than having been drawn from scripture. Pause for a moment and ask yourself: what does the way I live say about what I believe about God and what he requires of *me*? What do I believe in practice, not just in theory?

We want to bring honour to the Lord by our good works. We are concerned to protect his name from being dishonoured by our failings. But what starts out as a worthy concern can deteriorate into a sort of window-dressing exercise. Only those aspects of our individual or corporate life which we believe to be honouring to God are allowed to appear in the window, and everything else is kept firmly under wraps in the back room. Under these conditions appearances become inordinately important, and the fear of being found out grows as the gap between image and reality widens. It's rather like standing with one foot on the jetty and the other on a boat drifting away downstream. However much poise we may have succeeded in displaying, an undignified loss of face can't be far away! One day we'll be found out, that's for certain.

Many of us are vulnerable because of the value we place on other people's approval. Sometimes this amounts to a compulsion to please everyone. Church leaders who have little sense of their own worth in God's sight can overvalue popular acceptance of their ministry to such an extent that they develop a chameleon-like character, serially reflecting the many colours of opinion within their church. I have been told that when a chameleon is placed on a vividly patterned cloth made up of many different colours, it can't cope. If you're a pastor or church leader, you probably know the feeling! Trying to serve the Lord faithfully *and* keep everyone happy simultaneously doesn't work—in fact it often leads to paralysing indecision or accusations of compromise, or both! Paul's letter to the Galatians gives valuable insight. 'If I were still trying to please men, I would not be a servant of Christ,' he writes (Galatians 1:10).

God does not award prizes for window-dressing competitions or popularity contests. So why do we sometimes behave as if he did? God knows how many hours there are in a day, and how many of them need to be spent asleep. This being so, why do we live as if he were calling us to accomplish more than the time available could possibly accommodate? Is it possible that we're being driven beyond God's call, using 'church' to take our minds off the unease or pain that others dull with drink, drugs, extra-marital sex or loud pop music?

Drawing on both secular and Christian writing on addictions and addiction-driven lifestyles, I've sought to explain how unmet childhood needs and unresolved issues in our lives can lead to church activities and good works being pursued addictively or compulsively—how we can be serving our own needs rather than serving God. I've outlined the practical problems, especially for church leaders, and attempted to uncover the roots of drivenness and people-pleasing which, if not dealt with, can have a malignant effect on all our lives. I've posed questions designed to challenge the way we 'do church', and to highlight the need for healthy church communities within which needy folk are offered a remedy —not just an anaesthetic—for their pain.

We all have unmet needs, and no one's life is totally pain-free. It's not a sin to be needy or in pain. But the ways in which we try to meet the needs or to dull the pain can be sinful—contrary to God's will and purpose, neglecting the provisions he has already made for our legitimate needs. Where deep inner wounds have been driving ever more frantically towards an addictive substitute, the gracious Holy Spirit brings healing, renewal and an intimate relationship with 'the One and Only'. Rhythms of grace can replace the frenzy of drivenness. Where scripture has been misunderstood or distorted, the Truth himself can and does set free.

Yes, we'd probably all prefer to be popular. Yes, I dare say we're all tempted to try to 'look good while living lousy', especially if we're afraid that we might otherwise be letting the Lord down. But the consequences of allowing these concerns to steer our lives are serious. Jesus showed what it is to live a life of true communion with the Father, with no gap between the outer appearance and the inner reality. Jesus encourages us to walk that same road, even though our inner reality contains much of which we are rightly ashamed. Was Jesus popular? Some of the time. Did it hurt when the crowds turned against him? I'm sure it did. Did he allow concerns about popularity to set his agenda? I can find no evidence that he did.

Did you notice the verse of scripture at the beginning of this introduction, and the distorted way in which its meaning was reflected in the first paragraph? Love for God *will* (or should) result in service, but if service takes the central place in our lives which should be reserved for God, this is a form of idolatry. If we're truly loving God with all our heart, soul, mind and strength, service will be part—but *only* part—of the outworking of our growing relationship with him.

A right view of God and what he requires of us is essential for mental and spiritual health. God looks for an integrated spirituality, an all-pervading aroma which fragrances every part of life. He doesn't say: 'Here's a list of jobs to do—come back when you've finished and I'll give you another one.' Rather he says: 'Walk with me and work with me,' seeking to draw us into a relationship of love and service, a relationship within which we can grow in experience and maturity. Once secure in this relationship, other people's approval or disapproval matters less.

Whilst writing this book, I came across *The Message*'s version of the verses which are more familiar as 'Come to me, all you who are weary... Take my yoke upon you and learn from me...' (Matthew 11:28–29). Eugene Peterson's idiomatic translation, from which the phrase 'walk with me and work with me' is taken, has encouraged me as I've sought to discover the rhythms of grace for my own life. Are you prepared to take time to reflect on the pace, direction and motivation of *your* life? If so, read on...

Chapter 1 is a brief guided tour around the subject of addiction and drivenness in general. Other chapters then consider how the principles might be applied to churches and to the lives of individual Christians. *Focus points* at the end of each chapter encourage a pause for reflection before moving on to another topic. This is a worthwhile discipline, and of particular relevance to anyone seriously seeking to discover the rhythms of grace. If you find yourself wanting to skip the *Focus points*, please pause long enough to consider why!

# 1

# What's driving you?

*The Queen kept crying 'Faster! Faster!' ... 'Well, in our country,' said Alice, still panting a little, 'you'd generally get to somewhere else—if you ran very fast for a long time as we've been doing.' 'A slow sort of country!' said the Queen. 'Now, here, you see, it takes all the running you can do, to keep in the same place. If you want to get somewhere else, you must run at least twice as fast as that!'*

Lewis Carroll, *Through the Looking Glass*

I'm sometimes asked where drivenness ends and addiction begins. I don't find this an easy question to answer, and I'm not even sure that the answer is important because both are harmful. Perhaps people ask the question because they would prefer to think of themselves as driven rather than as addicted.

What picture does the word *addict* bring to your mind? Perhaps you think of a scruffy, shifty-eyed individual who makes you quicken your step and tighten your grip on your bag. But addicts come in all shapes and sizes, and many of them don't fit the traditional mental picture. In 1995 a general practitioner who had acted as adviser to the Thatcher government on its health service reforms was convicted of drug offences. He admitted that he had been injecting heroin up to eight times per day while advising the government. Although holding down a very responsible job, he used drugs from the age of seventeen until, in his mid-forties, he was charged with obtaining heroin by deception.

Those who use heroin regularly clearly have a problem. But what about the friend whom you seldom see because his job seems to demand more and more of his waking time, while his wife shops 'til she drops and his son plays on his computer? Perhaps you have a neighbour who is always on a diet, and who spends hours each week at the gym. Her shapely curves turn lots of heads, but she never seems satisfied with her figure—or her weight.

What about people you know whose lives seem to be driven by a single overwhelming concern? Some driving concerns are laudable—for example, the welfare of famine victims—some are less laudable, even laughable (such as collecting hundreds of garden gnomes). Would you go so far as to call these people addicts, because they allow their lives to be dominated by the pursuit of something damaging, or are totally given over to a harmless activity taken to unhealthy extremes?

# Definitions

The word addiction comes from the Latin word *addictus* which can be translated *given over*. This meaning comes from the Roman law courts, where a debtor could be given over to his creditor to act as a slave. The word dependency can be used as an alternative to addiction. It's seen as a less antagonistic word, but in practice the meaning is much the same.

The word *addict* has traditionally been used of a person who is dependent on drugs. As understanding of addictions has grown, it has become obvious that many people who do not use drugs experience similar 'highs' from other activities. Instead of chemicals they use computer games, keep-fit, romance, relationships, sex, worrying, shopping, gambling, work… some even use thinking, planning, day-dreaming about work (or one of the other activities) without actually doing very much of it. These are known as the process addictions, to distinguish them from the others which are known as chemical, substance, or ingestive addictions.

A wide variety of activities can alter our mood—by producing a feeling of well-being, or by blocking out troublesome feelings which might otherwise be clamouring for attention. It's so easy for use to slide into misuse and abuse. *Anything* that's used to alter our mood or block out troublesome feelings is potentially addictive.

# Dependency

Why do some individuals become dependent on drugs or processes when others don't? Not everyone who works hard becomes a workaholic. Many people take up keep-fit without becoming keep-fit addicts, and the majority of those who have a flutter on the Grand National seem able to do so without getting hooked on backing a winner. A quick puff behind the bike-shed at school doesn't automatically turn someone into a lifelong smoker. Not all teenagers who experiment with drugs go rapidly downhill and drop out of school.

## *Needing an anaesthetic*

In general, people are more likely to get hooked on a drug or a process if it has the effect of temporarily anaesthetizing them to long-standing inner pain of some sort. (A high proportion of drug addicts have been abused by those close to them. This happens in 'good, middle-class families' and among the materially wealthy, not just in economically deprived families.) If the pain goes for a while, whatever they have used feels like the answer they've been looking for. Once they've begun to use something as an escape, stopping doesn't feel like an option because this would allow the pain to return. A heavy smoker who is trying to give up is not good company! Neither is a workaholic on holiday (although some 'solve' this problem by taking a mobile phone and a laptop with them).

Some drugs actually alter the body's metabolism (for example: narcotics, alcohol) so that when the supply comes to an end the body reacts adversely to the change and there are physical withdrawal symptoms; other drugs do not affect the body's functioning in this way. However, research has shown that it's not simply the chemical or metabolic effect of a drug which impacts the body, leaving it vulnerable to physical symptoms on withdrawal: the circumstances associated with acquiring and taking a drug can affect brain chemistry by stimulating the release of natural substances in the body called *endorphins*. As it happens, the effects of endorphins are similar to those of heroin, so an addict will experience something of a high—even if the powder purchased has been heavily diluted with an inert substance, or contains no heroin at all.

Whilst endorphin research is of interest to those studying addictions, endorphins have much wider relevance, and contribute significantly to the body's ability to respond appropriately to a range of non-drug-related circumstances. For example, they are released naturally in the body during physical exercise, which may go some way to explaining its addictive potential.

It's important to recognize that for some folk the sense of rewarding themselves with whatever it is they're taking may be just as important as the substance used. Chocolate can be seen as a mood-altering substance, but for some chocoholics the sense of being nice to themselves is much more important than any chemical activity it may have. For some smokers the process of taking time out and giving themselves the gift of a cigarette will be just as difficult to give up as the nicotine intake.

Speaking more generally, withdrawal can bring loneliness, and a sense of desolation without the all-consuming focus—whatever it was. If a person's life has revolved around keep-fit, drinking or obtaining drugs, their significant relationships are likely to be with others who are doing the same. Relationships with non-participating family members and old friends may well have broken up— because they've found the addict's behaviour unacceptable, or because the addict has preferred to mix with fellow junkies. This makes the way back to a life without the addiction very hard indeed.

## From one thing to another

Another important aspect of dependency is the doubling up and swapping around. A workaholic may insist that she doesn't have a problem because she never takes work home. And it may be true that she doesn't take work home! But isn't she spending every spare second of daylight caring for her prize-winning roses? And during the winter, doesn't she pass the long, dark evenings immersed in her stamp collection? What is it that's so painful that she can't afford to have an idle moment lest it break through into her consciousness?

A drug addict may try to convince himself and others that he is cured because he's off drugs. But if he's filling the gap with alcohol, or has become a 'respectable' workaholic who uses prostitutes when away from home on business trips, he's still in deep trouble—different trouble, but just as deep. Some people spend their lives going from one source of highs to another, leaving broken relationships and faded hopes in their wake.

Suzanne came to see me for counselling after she had given up drinking alcohol and joined a church. She had really taken to her new-found friends, and called them often on the phone, dropping round to see them whenever she could. She also kept in touch with her old friends from her drinking days, not wanting to upset them by making a clean break with her old way of life.

She found it quite difficult to fit in counselling appointments, what with church events, house group meetings, helping those in need, and not wanting to say 'No' to her long-standing friends. She found work for the first time for ages, and embarked on it with considerable enthusiasm and optimism. This was going to be the start of a whole new life full of opportunities. She began to worry about her weight, which was creeping up. Suzanne ate in order to feel good, and then worried about her figure. She would have liked to have given up smoking, but was sure that this would only lead to more weight gain.

Once Suzanne started work, time was at a premium, and soon counselling appointments could no longer be fitted into her schedule. Then church activities tailed off, as she spent more time with her old friends. Some months later I heard that she had lost her job because of a drinking binge. A few months after that, I heard that she had joined another church, where she was rapidly becoming fully involved.

## Is there such a thing as a good addiction?

Isn't it better to be addicted to sport or religion than to drugs or alcohol? Surely it can't be right to speak in the same breath of addiction to sex and addictions to keep-fit or work? How can such depravity be put alongside an activity which develops and finetunes the body, or one which yields an honest living and provides for the needs of a family?

There is nothing wrong with keep-fit, work or belonging to a church, any more than there is with sex—all are God-given. But all can be abused as part of an addictive process.

Carl Jung, the Swiss psychologist, observed that all addictions are 'bad', whether the chosen drug be alcohol, morphine or idealism. There is no such thing as a good addiction, and swapping to one which is more socially acceptable is not the same as giving up, coming off the hook.

# Features of addiction

These may be seen in the lives of addicts, but they may also be seen in the lives of a large number of other fragile human beings who choose to meet their needs in ways which are less obviously self-destructive. Not everyone who has these problems is an addict, but they may be a pointer to unresolved difficulties needing attention.

As a part of growing to maturity, we can all benefit from reflecting on the methods we are using to cope with those aspects of our lives which we find painful or difficult. The question isn't simply: 'Are we addicts, yes or no?' Rather, we need to ask ourselves how we deal with our pain. Do we acknowledge our discomfort—or do we try to drown it? To what extent is unacknowledged pain in the driving seat of our lives?

What follows is a brief tour around some of the important features of addiction. For convenience I've divided them into five main problem areas: self-esteem, identity, physical effects, psychological features, and spiritual bankruptcy. Not all the features described will be present in every case, although most are more common than we might expect.

# Self-esteem problems

Some individuals are able to hear affirming words from friends or colleagues without receiving even a grain of encouragement, because they're sure that the nice things being said can't possibly be true. Deep down they just *know* they're worthless failures. If a few kind folk say encouraging things about them it just goes to show that it's possible to fool some of the people some of the time.

Having no sense of our own worth is usually due to some childhood needs not having been met. These needs include: security—knowing our survival is not in jeopardy; a sense of belonging, and being accepted for who we are; and a growing sense of our own competence. God's plan is that these needs are met for children in families. The reasons for them not being met are many and varied. Some children are actively abused or wilfully neglected by their parents, who may be repeating the treatment they themselves received at the hand of their own parents. Other children suffer neglect due to one or both parents working very long hours, being physically absent due to evening commitments, or emotionally absent due to exhaustion.

## Parents can be doing their best

In some cases, the parents are doing the very best they can under very difficult circumstances, such as coping with serious physical or mental illness, perhaps culminating in the death of one parent. Recurring or chronic unemployment may necessitate uprooting the family in order to find work. We are still seeing the legacies of the upheaval brought about by World War II—absence on military service for the father, evacuation of individual children or part-families, deprivation, daily confrontations with the horrors of death and destruction and so on. The insecurity caused by disruptions to the formative years of an earlier generation continues to exert an effect even today in some families.

It is frequently said that children are good recorders but poor interpreters. Whilst more or less correctly registering the disturbing things they see and hear going on around them, they can still go on to draw the wrong conclusions. Children often mistakenly believe that unpleasant things which happen around them are their fault. They may blame themselves for the death of one of their parents, or the chronic illness of a brother or sister. They can feel responsible for difficulties in their parents' marriage. I was in my early forties when I suddenly realized that I had always blamed myself for my mother's depression. I had somehow come to believe it was all my fault.

## Shaky foundations for adulthood

If basic needs are not met, or damaging beliefs about their own 'badness' are stored and carried, children may grow into adults with shaky foundations and a very distorted view of themselves. They may be unable to believe that anyone could possibly like or accept them as they are. People are very kind to bother with them, they say to themselves, fearing that those who speak pleasantly to them are doing so out of pity—and probably saying less complimentary things when out of earshot.

Children who have not developed a sense of their own competence will grow into adults who are incapable of making a realistic assessment of their own abilities. They may appear full of confidence for a while, taking on commitments and speaking boldly about their capabilities, only to disappear into a pit of gloom in which they lament the foolish conceit which allowed them to believe they could do anything at all. Often the optimism expressed at their high points is as unreal as the pessimism of the low points: they just don't know how to appraise their own capabilities. Others are more consistent, always seeing themselves as worthless and useless—'a waste of space'—however much they achieve in the eyes of those around them.

They may prefer to rely on others to tell them what to think, feel and do, because they are sure they can't be trusted to get it right. They will find it hard to say 'No' to people, reasoning that if someone else thinks a course of action is a good idea they should agree and say 'Yes', whatever their own thoughts and feelings about it. Chronic low-level anxiety may lurk in the background, as they're sure they're going to find something they can't deal with around the next corner. One response is to try to meet every fear before it arises, living a highly controlled and restricted life and venturing nothing, in order not to be overwhelmed by unknown possibilities for failure.

A childhood in which needs are not met stores up a lot of pain which cannot safely be expressed and dealt with at the time. In later life, an addiction may be used as an anaesthetic for the stored emotional pain. It doesn't solve anything but it dulls the ache. It's vital to look at the source of the pain rather than focusing on the addiction alone, otherwise the result may be apparent success but with no real change. A drug addict who gives up drugs and becomes a keep-fit addict may attract much worthy comment, and find herself more socially acceptable, but the pain is just the same. Same pain, different anaesthetic.

# Identity problems

A newborn baby has no real sense of where he begins and ends physically. He learns over the weeks and months that he can control, with increasing precision, those podgy pink things which wave about in front of his nose. He discovers that sucking them can be comforting. He also learns that those things which can be sucked in order to give a warm, full feeling in his midriff are not under his control—are not part of him—although persistent bellowing can usually bring results!

## *'Who am I?'*

Children also need to develop a growing sense of who they are as a person. As they mature, they need to become aware of boundaries between what is their responsibility and what is not. They need to be able to identify what they think, what they feel, and so on. They also need to know that thinking or feeling something different from someone else is not automatically wrong.

When people fall in love, they may find that there is an initial blurring of identity boundaries, so that they find they like the same music or food as their beloved, and modify their choice of clothes to emphasize that they are at one with each other. As love matures, it may be safe to disagree, but this is not so in some relationships, and one partner may end up sacrificing their identity in order to maintain the relationship.

Children coming from families in which it is regarded as disloyal or in some other way unsafe to think or feel differently may never develop a full sense of their personhood. As they grow up, they won't see themselves as unique individuals with a valid contribution to make to the world around them, and their own unique furrow to plough. Their answer to the question 'Who am I?' may be 'I wish someone would tell me!' They will tend to look outside themselves for answers to questions like 'How am I doing?' and 'Where am I going?'

Even as full-grown adults, they will attach considerable importance to the views and feelings of others. They may not even know how to think their own thoughts or feel their own feelings. They'll wait for others to express their point of view so that they know what to say. If others are happy, sad or angry, they'll feel the same. However, true empathy will be unknown to them, as this requires being in touch with their own feelings as well as those of another person.

## Difficulties with intimacy

People without a properly developed sense of their own identity are often well-practised at creating the right impression, presenting an image which corresponds to what they believe is required in order to gain acceptance. They are desperate to know that they're doing OK; they crave positive feedback, even if it's being given to their carefully constructed image rather than to the real person they are. Under these conditions, getting close is well nigh impossible. True closeness involves sharing the real self, rather than the image they want everyone to see. They may become expert at *pretending* closeness and sharing, while keeping the drawbridge in the up position.

Relationships can become a matter of *control*: I need to control what you think and feel about me, and preferably about everything else too, so that I can feel secure. If you don't oblige, I'll probably reject you in case you're about to reject me. I may opt for another relationship—one with someone who is only too happy to be controlled, and to think and feel to order. But what sort of a relationship will that be?

A lack of identity, the need to control, and the overwhelming craving for positive feedback make intimacy difficult. Harriet Goldhor Lerner writes:

> *Intimacy means that we can be who we are in a relationship, and allow the other person to do the same. 'Being who we are' requires that we can talk openly about things that are important to us, that we take a clear position on where we stand on important*

*emotional issues, and that we clarify the limits of what is accept-*
*able and tolerable to us in a relationship. 'Allowing the other per-*
*son to do the same' means that we can stay emotionally connected*
*to that other party who thinks, feels, and believes differently, with-*
*out needing to change, convince, or fix the other.*

Harriet Goldhor Lerner, *The Dance of Intimacy*

## Relationship addiction

Addicts of all sorts have problems with intimacy, but it would seem logical to assume that relationship addicts were an exception; this is not so. Relationship addicts are good at *simulating* intimacy, but are too vulnerable to go for the real thing. They are unlikely to *want* to be themselves in any relationship. Their priority is to sustain the relationship at all costs, so they will 'be' whatever is required.

There may be a strong fantasy element, perhaps fuelled by lonely hours spent reading Mills and Boon novels. Relationship addicts have such a compelling desire to keep the relationship going that they'll spend money they don't have, either to support the fantasy they've built up or to woo their would-be partner with gifts and surprises. The lack of *true* intimacy becomes apparent when the bubble bursts and the relationship breaks down. One moment the addict's whole world is coming to an end—all is lost, and life is no longer worth living; the next moment, they are rushing with little more than a backward glance into a new and equally all-consuming commitment.

# Physical effects

Where harmful substances are being used there will obviously be physical consequences. To add to that, habits which are expensive may lead to raising money through prostitution, and the risk of assault and sexually transmitted disease. Much violent crime is driven by the need to fund a drug habit or other addiction; those involved risk injury both from those they attack and from competing criminals. Addiction reduces life-expectancy and increases the risk of serious injury and illness.

## One-track minds

However, many of the physical consequences of addiction and drivenness are due to pervasive attitudes rather than dramatic events.
One of the quotable quotes in my diary tells me that John F.
Kennedy said: 'We must use time as a tool, not as a couch.' I don't
know the context within which he made this remark, but it could
be interpreted in several ways. A workaholic would see it as vindi-
cating his or her approach—always driving on, never wasting a
moment. But in fact the uses of time can include self-care activities such as eating and sleeping, as well as reflection, relationship
building... Can you think of some other important ways of using
time which don't always have an obvious point in the short term
but which show their value in the long term? Using time doesn't
need to mean rushing about doing things in the activist sense.
Indeed it *is* a tool, but that doesn't mean it can't be used for anything other than work, whatever a workaholic might say!

Serious gamblers seem to think that money exists only to
be used as a stake! The supposedly harmless-bit-of-fun National
Lottery has brought tales of families going without food and other
necessities. Some even risk imprisonment for not paying their rent
or community charge, in order to fund a substantial twice-weekly
stake. People who are driven or addicted have a different perspective on things which others see as normal and ordinary, such as
eating, sleeping and paying bills.

## Self-neglect

Self-esteem problems, and most addictions, are accompanied by a
degree of self-neglect. For addicts of all sorts, poor nutrition and
erratic sleep patterns are more or less normal. A proper diet takes
not only money but time—time which someone with a single driving concern may be reluctant to give, especially if they don't believe they're worth caring for. The idea of winding down at the end
of the day in preparation for bed seems to be unknown to many
who wouldn't see themselves as driven let alone addicted! It's not
logical to expect to fall soundly asleep as soon as our head hits the
pillow, regardless of what has been happening all day and all
evening. Frenzied days usually lead to restless nights.

Physical fitness addicts may be less prone to nutritional problems, but may neglect wider aspects of physical well-being in the
pursuit of particular goals. They are at risk of over-use injuries and
'burn-out', and may be lured into taking harmful drugs to en-
hance their performance.

### Accidents happen—more often

No one is immune to accidental injury and accidental death, but
some people make themselves more vulnerable by their chosen
lifestyle. There may be obvious cause and effect in drug addicts,
in whom an accidental or intentional overdose may be fatal.
However, other addicts, such as gamblers and users of prostitutes,
and even 'respectable' addicts, such as workaholics, may lay themselves open to accidents too. This may be due to being mentally
preoccupied, for example when driving (in which case others
may also be injured, perhaps fatally). The characteristic haste when
looking to 'score' can lead to the neglect of common-sense safety
precautions (for example, when crossing the road to the betting
shop).

Chronic exhaustion opens the door to a wide range of physical
ills in addition to accidents. This applies to all causes of exhaustion, including some which seem unavoidable, such as caring for
a sick child or an elderly relative, not just drivenness. However,
those who do not value their own well-being, or who are trying
hard to numb their inner pain with drugs or activities, will be
particularly vulnerable.

# Psychological features

It's no surprise that addicts suffer from psychological problems.
Some of them pre-date the addiction, whilst others are as a result
of it. But addicts do not hold the monopoly on these problems,
and some may sound remarkably familiar!

### Swinging moods

Mood swings (alternating highs and lows), and irritability with outbursts of temper, could be pointers to a problem which is otherwise being kept under wraps. A workaholic I once knew was held

in high regard by those around him, who were totally thrown by his occasional flips into rage mode. They saw these as out of character, when in fact they were pointers towards an inner reality which he preferred to keep hidden.

## Compulsions

The term 'obsessive compulsive behaviour' covers a wide variety of patterns, which can be anything from trivial to life-disrupting. These include incessant hand-washing, an obsession with cleanliness, checking that the back door is locked numerous times each night, feeling compelled to say a particular prayer in a particular way or to go through some other ritual many times each day. Obsessive compulsive disorders are more common amongst those suffering from an addiction, as are phobias (irrational fears), but non-addicts can suffer from them too.

## Disabling the able

Many people, including addicts, suffer from poor concentration and impaired judgment. Besides affecting personal relationships, these can lead to getting the sack from work, or to business failure if the affected person is in a responsible position. An addict may become mentally preoccupied with where their next fix is coming from, and may be sufficiently desperate to leave work in the middle of a crucial deal, or to gloss over important aspects of a contract, in order to take an early lunch and 'score'. (This applies to those who are in the grip of process addictions. It is not just associated with popping pills or alcohol.)

It's important to be aware that the pull of process addictions is sufficient to disable otherwise very able individuals. For example, a businessman who uses prostitutes addictively can be just as unreliable as an alcoholic, and just as driven in his craving as a heroin addict, abandoning all else in the pursuit of relief. When British climber Alison Hargreaves died in 1995, attempting to conquer Mount Everest, there was much written in the newspapers about how easy it is for even experienced climbers to push on beyond what their otherwise sound judgment would say is safe, driven by their desire to get to the top.

## *Risk-taking and sensation-seeking*

It is probably true that some people's personalities make them more vulnerable to addictions. Certainly, those who have a sensation-seeking disposition will crave arousing experiences, and are likely to be drawn to anything new and exciting, pushing themselves further in the pursuit of the ultimate buzz, even if there are obvious risks attached. However, personality is never the only factor in the equation: a person who feels that they are a waste of space and that no one cares for them is likely to express their personality in more dangerous or potentially self-destructive ways than someone who knows that they are loved.

The degree of risk-taking varies. It may simply be the risk of being thought rather foolish, or it may amount to the risk of losing everything—job, reputation, marriage... Addicts risk ill-health and their own lives, but may also risk the health and welfare of others. A wife might unwittingly risk catching AIDS or other sexually-transmitted diseases if her husband is using prostitutes compulsively. A woman who is selling her body to fund an expensive habit risks infecting her husband, and may be putting her children's safety at risk too. Where large sums of money are required to resource an addiction or a driven lifestyle, the family home may be at risk because of mounting debts, having been re-mortgaged without the rest of the family's knowledge. Families who thought that insurance would cover mortgage and other payments in the event of the death of the main bread-winner could find themselves in dire straits if he or she dies from a cause which is excluded in a policy.

Risks may be taken solely in order to obtain the fix, or an element of risk (for example, *unprotected* sex, rather than just illicit sex) may be added specifically in order to heighten the thrill, as part of sensation-seeking. It is difficult to understand why apparently rational people in responsible positions will risk everything in pursuit of a craving, but some do. In 1991 the then Director of Public Prosecutions lost everything because he was caught trying to pick up a prostitute. He must have known that he could be spotted by the police, and he would have been well able to foresee the consequences for a man with his legal responsibilities, but he still went ahead and did it. Sadly, from time to time well-respected folk in public and church life attract media attention when they behave in ways which are seen as totally out of character. The very real risk of exposure may have been contributing to the buzz they were getting from the activity or drugs in which they were secretly indulging.

On a more mundane level, I would urge everyone to reflect on their style of driving. While steadying myself by hanging on to the door handle and wondering why I agreed to the offer of a lift, I've observed the tremendous adrenaline rush some people seem to get by pushing their vehicles, not to mention the rules of the road, up to and sometimes beyond reasonable limits. Leaving later than common sense would dictate (to ensure an even greater surge of adrenaline?) they have driven furiously to the destination, showing little regard for other road users. I think of one mild-mannered church leader who was transformed into a veritable Ben Hur when he took to the road. He clearly enjoyed the adrenaline rush which the journey provoked in a way that I did not!

## *Denial*

Denial is a *defence mechanism*. When we find something deeply disturbing we can deny that it exists. This is not a clearly thought-out process, and if others challenge us to admit whatever it is we are denying we may sincerely believe that they're mistaken. Although there may be some overlap with lying (as described later) it's important to differentiate it. Someone who is in denial about their problem-drinking may believe that you're imagining that they have a problem. Someone who denies having stopped off at the pub on the way to meet you (even though you saw them do so) is lying, unless, for example, chronic alcoholism is causing blackouts, so that they have no idea where they've been for the past few hours.

Denial may be straightforward: 'I haven't had a fix for ages.' Denial by comparison or trade-off is more subtle, and can even be associated with a faint air of martyrdom. This may prompt whoever raised the subject to back off, feeling a bit guilty. For example, a workaholic might say to his family: 'Sure you don't see much of me, but at least I'm working hard to give us a good standard of living rather than drinking our money away at the pub with the other lads.' A woman might remind her husband that, although she spends a lot of time at the fitness centre, it would be embarrassing for him if he had a wife who had 'gone to seed'. Denial may include using others as scapegoats to take the blame. For example: 'I only drink because you nag', or 'I wouldn't have to work so hard if you weren't so extravagant'.

### *Redefining normal*

The most pernicious form of denial, in my view, is denial by *redefining normal*. This messes up those around the addict, and is a factor in transmitting addiction-related behaviour down the generations. For example: 'It's normal to go straight to the betting shop on pay-day, and to end up living on bread and butter and pretending you're out when the milkman calls for his money.' In some families it's normal for mum or dad to say they're coming to Sports Day and Parents' Evening and to have a really 'good' reason why, at the last minute, they couldn't make it. Every year. You probably wouldn't agree that it's normal to take work with you on holiday, unless of course you've had your norms realigned by living with a workaholic.

It's amazing what some people will try to pass off as normal. Recently on television a man was explaining to a group of drug addicts how his wife's thinking needed to be unscrambled when he gave up drinking. Feeling rather like Alice in *Through the Looking Glass*, she had come to accept that, whatever her view of reality, others saw it differently. She had come to the point where she no longer saw it as peculiar to find a bottle of gin in the cistern of the toilet. Now, if she'd found a bottle of *milk* in the cistern, she'd have known something was wrong, but he'd convinced her that gin in the cistern was OK.

# Spiritual bankruptcy

I first came across the expression 'spiritual bankruptcy' in Diane Fassel's book *Working Ourselves to Death*. It paints such a vivid image for the Christian, even if the phrase was not coined with a specifically Christian meaning in mind. It does not refer to a person's failure to keep a set of externally-imposed rules or standards.

We are spiritually bankrupt when we break *whatever moral code we have chosen to live by*, when we go against *our own value system*.

For example, in order to buy drugs an addict may be driven to prostitution or robbery with violence, even though he or she believes these to be morally wrong. A teenage fruit-machine gambler, stealing in order to fund his addiction, may be desperate enough to steal his own granny's purse—and then go on to convince her she must have lost it. In so doing he violates his value system which gives a high priority to the family, especially its senior members, or says that it's wrong to abuse vulnerable people. A relationship addict may consent to sexual intercourse rather than risk losing this month's man of her dreams, even though this goes against her religious beliefs.

## *Lying and deceiving*

Anyone who has lived with someone in the grip of an addiction knows that lying and deceiving can become a way of life—even for those who would previously have regarded this as totally unacceptable. Anne Wilson Schaeff writes:

> *An addiction is any process over which we are powerless. It takes control of us, causing us to do and think things that are inconsistent with our personal values and leading us to become progressively more compulsive and obsessive. A sure sign of an addiction is the sudden need to deceive ourselves and others—to lie, deny and cover up. An addiction is anything we feel tempted to lie about.*

Anne Wilson Schaeff, *When Society Becomes an Addict*

One lie can so easily lead to another. We may call it bending the truth, being economical with the truth, sparing those we love the agony of knowing the full facts—'Didn't want to worry you, dear'—but, by any other name, it's lying. The lying may involve our use of time, or our money—perhaps leading to the mysterious disappearance of bank or credit card statements in an attempt to conceal transactions associated with the addiction or obsession.

The deception may also involve our thoughts drifting far away when we're on holiday, or our affections being focused elsewhere while we are physically going through the motions of making love with our spouse. Some take the view that their thoughts are their own, and that provided they're not acting upon them no harm is being done. This does not appear to be Jesus' view (see Matthew 5:28).

It's important to realize that the lying of an addict may be so extraordinary that it is difficult to accept that a person would say such a thing unless they believed it to be true. This may be because of the seriousness of the lying (for example, blaming others for major wrongdoing of which they are genuinely innocent) or the absolute certainty of being found out before very long.

Marilyn had worked happily for several years as book-keeper to a small family business. She became uneasy after a new office manager was appointed, although she found it difficult to put her finger on the problem. She decided she needed to be vigilant, especially with regard to the financial transactions for which she and the office manager shared responsibility. From time to time the manager was absent from work without warning. Marilyn found that his subsequent explanations did not ring true, although no one else shared her misgivings.

One morning, the staff were shocked to hear that the manager was absent from work because his daughter had been killed in an accident. Messages of sympathy and flowers were sent, and everyone shared a sense of loss. Later that week, Marilyn happened to be visiting a friend who lived a few doors away from the manager, and remarked about the tragedy. The friend looked at her as if she had taken leave of her senses, and pointed to the man's daughter who was playing in the street. It turned out that the manager was an alcoholic. His absences from work were due to drinking bouts, but people had believed his other explanations. Their suspicions had not been aroused and so they had accepted what he said at face value.

## *Promising*

Promising is a form of lying at which addicts excel. The need for impression management is strong, and saying what people want to hear is one way to create a good impression. If I'm enslaved by an addiction I may make promises I know I haven't the power to keep, such as 'Never again'. I may even make promises that I know I don't have the remotest intention of keeping, in order to keep people happy, however temporarily. Breaking promises made for keeps is the other side of the coin. Marriage vows, however sincerely meant at the time, can fall victim to spiritual bankruptcy.

If we live a life which is in breach of our own value system, causing distress to those around us by lying and breaking promises, this will add to our existing difficulties with self-worth and increase the load of pain which we're trying to anaesthetize in unhealthy ways. This will drive us further down the same path.

Having taken a panoramic view of the landscape of addiction, the focus now moves to the church. In order to be able to minister freedom to those in the grip of addiction and drivenness, the church may first need to put her own house in order. However, before rushing on, the *Focus point* which follows gives an opportunity to reflect further on some of the issues raised in this chapter, as does Study 1 at the end of the book.

# Focus point

**'Who or what is at the centre of my life—as I live it, not as I theorize about it?'**

Take time to answer this question. You may find the following additional questions helpful.

Look through your diary or calendar—but not simply at the time you spend on different activities. Ask yourself: **'What would I always manage to find space for, even if it meant cancelling something else?'**

**'What do I spend most of my time thinking about?'** If you're standing in a long queue, or doing a task which doesn't require much mental effort, where do your thoughts end up?

**'What would those nearest and dearest to me say if I asked them to list my priorities?'**

# The religious fix

## Jonah 2:8

*Those who cling to worthless idols*
*forfeit the grace that could be theirs.*

Much has been said about the spiritual vacuum of our day which leads spiritually hungry people to try almost anything that promises to take away the ache in their souls. It may be less obvious that some folk within our churches are equally needy—we may assume that because they're in church their spiritual needs are being met appropriately, but it's possible to use the *process* of meeting with or serving God in such a way that it takes on all the characteristics of an addiction.

In the wilderness, Jesus reminded Satan that it is written: 'Worship the Lord your God, and serve him only' (Matthew 4:10). We are to worship God, not the church or even, dare I say it, the Bible. There are different Greek words in the New Testament for worship. One is *latreuo* which can also be translated *serve*. The addict both serves and worships the addictive substance or process, and this is grace-forfeiting idolatry even if the process has religious connections.

## Using 'church'

People can use the process of 'doing church' to dull their inner pain. We do well to ask ourselves from time to time: 'Am I willing to examine my Christian life and service for signs of being driven by unacknowledged neediness—rather than being called and led by God?'

For example, is my church life lived at workaholic pace? If so, why? What need—whose need—is this meeting? Could my strong leadership be driven by a need to control (in order to feel the security which was lacking in childhood) rather than empowered by the Holy Spirit? Do I put so much effort into pastoral care because of an overwhelming need to be needed? Do I only sense God's love when I'm helping others? Am I only aware of his presence when I'm leading a service? Why do I go to church? Is it primarily to worship God, or for some other reason?

Are the many strands of my life (work, church, family, friends...) straining so hard in opposing directions that I feel as if I'm about to be pulled limb from limb? Is my life like the plate-spinning act—running frantically from one to the other just in time to stop them from crashing, but never pausing long enough anywhere to reflect on what I'm doing? If so, why do I choose to live like this?

## 'But I can't stop'

The thought of stopping can provoke anxiety—not least because we fear that so much that is good might be left undone. A healthy response to such a concern might be to pause and reflect. Realistically, we may not be able to see how the job could possibly get done without us. Eddie Askew of The Leprosy Mission captures the dilemma and suggests a new perspective:

> *I buzz around, a frantic fly*
> *battering the window pane*
> *until I fall exhausted to the sill.*
> *All noise and movement but so little done.*
> *And in the effort to respond*
> *to all the calls that others make*
> *I find I'm losing touch with you.*
> *The crowds get in between.*
> *The more I do for you*
> *the further off you seem.*

*A paradox until I hear your voice,*
*not asking more of me*
*but telling me to find a breathing space,*
*a place to rest...*

*You made the world,*
*it wasn't me*
*and, valued as I am,*
*it's you who keeps it going.*

Eddie Askew, *Cross Purposes:*
*Meditations and prayers based on meals with Jesus*

Perhaps there *are* others waiting in the wings to do the jobs we need to lay down, or who would willingly come alongside to share the load if only they knew... Perhaps there needs to be a gap for a while, for reasons we can't yet see. Perhaps some of the roles we play are no longer part of God's plan. Perhaps all this sounds too simplistic and naïve!

The bottom line is that God is not daft. He knows how many hours there are in a day, and how many days there are in a week. He also knows that we don't have endless energy, and that out of each twenty-four hours some need to be spent asleep. Logically, he will not ask us to do so much that we require ten-day weeks with forty-eight-hour days to get it all done. So, if it's not God who's driving us into the ground, who or what is?

## *What would I be doing if I weren't...*

We all have a capacity for self-deception. We need to be willing to ask ourselves if our hectic lifestyle is really a sign of wholehearted Christian commitment, or a pointer to something else. Could there be a pay-off we've not recognized? Have we become hooked on the adrenaline of endless crises? How would we feel about ourselves if we didn't have so many important hats to wear? What would we be facing up to at home if we weren't always out?

It might seem logical to assume that someone who is a faithful attender at every church prayer meeting is devoted to prayer. The reality may be that he or she is using attendance at prayer meetings as a way of dulling the pain of disintegrating relationships at home —and an opportunity to escape from a difficult environment. Yes, it can be good to take time out from our own concerns in order to pray for others. But prayer needs to be a way of engaging with difficulties, and praying for God's will to be done in and through them. It should not be primarily an escape route or a distraction which allows us to pretend that they do not exist.

I have tried to keep on asking myself: 'What would I be doing if I weren't writing?' At times there has been a strong temptation to retreat into book-writing, using it as a welcome escape from the normal hurly-burly of living with adolescents and a husband! I make it a rule to take a regular day off each week—in addition to Sundays. I also make it a rule not to write in the evenings. This is partly because writing is an anti-social activity which shuts out other people, but also because I know that if my brain has been humming with interesting ideas all evening I won't be able to get to sleep.

## Desperately seeking...

When desperate and needy individuals come to church, are they seeking Christ, or seeking relief? Some come with such burdens and pain that they would be prepared to take any answer. We need to make sure that they receive Christ as Saviour, Redeemer, Son of the Living God, rather than fixing on church or religion as some sort of cure-all pill or anaesthetic.

As a teenager I spent a lot of time in church activities. I valued the friendships of other young people (in those days the only social gatherings for teenagers of both sexes were church youth groups!) and the numerous activities which were arranged. I enjoyed the sense of belonging, and the appreciation of what I was able to contribute. It was somewhere I could go and be 'me', a vital part of adolescence.

Rather than going on to develop a relationship with Jesus, I could have pinned all my hopes on the youth group and church. And they would have let me down. For many folk the church offers relief from loneliness and insignificance, supplying a ready-filled calendar of activities and a long list of good works needing to be done. If people are using church as an anaesthetic for their personal pain, sooner or later the church will let them down. Is it possible that some of the discontent voiced in churches is because the church (or the church leader) has been expected to meet needs which God alone is able to meet?

## Come and join us

When I was at medical school I was uncomfortable with the apparent drivenness of some of the student evangelism I saw around me. Probably much of it was motivated by nothing more sinister than youthful enthusiasm. But maybe some of it was driven by the needs of those involved rather than by a love of the Lord and a desire to share it. It's possible for evangelism to be pursued compulsively, as a way of meeting a need for significance.

Evangelism can even become an idol—especially successful evangelism! Those so evangelized may find Christ, but they may simply become entangled in a process which leads them to evangelize others. This is one of the marks of a cult. This is not an argument against evangelism *per se*. But Christians should not be using the process of evangelism primarily as a way to feel good about themselves or their church. I am also very concerned about evangelism which introduces people to church, a schedule of activities, and a list of right answers rather than to Christ himself.

From time to time, pausing and reviewing can be helpful. What has happened to those who have joined the church? (If no one *has* joined, why not?) Has the pace and focus of church life been such that, having wooed them in, we've then neglected them? Or even abused them by press-ganging them to join us on the treadmill?

## Addiction to religion

Anne Wilson Schaeff writes: 'The religion addict is very different, inside and out, from the person who is involved in spiritual growth. The religion addict loses touch with personal values and develops behaviours that are the same as those of the alcoholic or drug addict—judgmentalism, dishonesty, and control. Use moves into abuse' (Anne Wilson Schaeff, *When Society Becomes an Addict*).

It can be very difficult to pinpoint the exact moment at which church attendance becomes 'churchaholism', and indeed the early stages of churchaholism may not show the stark features described above. Geraldine was a lonely child, who joined a church youth group as a teenager. She became a faithful attender at church services. When she left home to go to university in a city about thirty miles away, she joined a large church which was led by a well-regarded preacher, and became fully involved. When Geraldine was at home with her parents during university holidays, she felt she had to spend a significant amount of money, as well as time, to return to the city for the whole day each Sunday— so that she could attend all the services at what was now her home church.

Geraldine also attended the youth club's mid-week prayer and Bible study meetings in her parents' town, but she found it very hard to fit in. She spent much of the time talking in glowing terms about how wonderful it was at the city church, and seemed unable to relate to anything that went on anywhere else. It was almost as if Geraldine had begun to worship the church in the city... The church itself had a strong biblical foundation, and I'm sure its leaders and members would have been horrified to think that their church was being used as part of an addictive process. Geraldine went on to develop severe housemaid's knee as a result of all the hours spent on her knees praying. Her life was very narrow, and seemed to include only academic study and religion.

At some point or other, Geraldine had crossed the line which separates commitment from obsession. It can be easier to spot the transition in retrospect, but often we know we had uneasy feelings at the time which we persuaded ourselves to ignore. Someone may have been trying to convince us that, because a certain amount of something is good, an even larger amount of it must be very good. We may find it hard to fault their reasoning, but at gut level we know there's something wrong.

Anglican minister and theologian Mark Stibbe writes:

> *The religious addict is someone whose primary goal is to obtain some form of mood-altering, emotional encounter in and through religion. Because the setting of this particular form of*

*addiction is a pious one (as opposed to a bar, a brothel, or a bet-*
*ting office, for example), the addict easily justifies the dependency.*
*Like the religious workaholic, the religious addict legitimizes*
*what is ultimately excessive and destructive behaviour.*

Mark Stibbe, *O Brave New Church:*
*rescuing the addictive culture*

Elsewhere in the same book, Stibbe comments on the number of
clergy who preach justification by faith and end up living 'justification by busyness'. This cannot fail to undermine their message.
In addition it can set an unhealthy pattern for the church, by
apparently legitimizing a gap between words and deeds.

## Being willing to be challenged

Are we willing to face up to the possibility that the church's message is being undermined by the way we go about things? In her
hard-hitting book, Diane Fassel writes:

*'Doing' religion workaholically is an assault on the very spir-*
*ituality the church promises. How can you teach 'life more abun-*
*dant' when you are working yourself to death?... No church*
*hiring committee would consider giving a job to an applicant who*
*was an active drug abuser. Why hire an active workaholic? Same*
*disease, same consequences, same loss of spirituality.*

Diane Fassel, *Working Ourselves to Death*

If an alcoholic were to join our church seeking recovery, is it possible that he might abandon alcohol because he gets caught up in
the heady pursuit of 100 per cent proof religion rather than because he meets with Jesus? Would an impartial outsider recognize
our worship services as opportunities to meet with the living
God, or would they lump them in with other mood-altering or
sensation-seeking activities which carry an addictive potential?
(We will discuss this further in chapter 5.) What about the
church's emphasis on doctrinal correctness, credal statements
and signed declarations from those seeking membership? Are
these in any danger of taking precedence over the sort of issues

(such as justice, mercy and faithfulness—see Matthew 23:23) which Jesus saw as of primary importance?

If our identity is to be found in our church membership, or in our leadership role, this will have consequences—for us, and for those around us. If our sense of being is found in our 'doing'—attending church and Christian meetings, doing good works and following an arduous schedule of personal devotions—we need to admit that we have a problem.

The Christian life is not a list to be lived (first giving to those who ask, second visiting those in prison, then praying for those who persecute us, and so on). It is a life in which every aspect of what we do and are is to be fragranced by God's presence, and from which service to others will flow as a consequence of our 'in-Christ-ness'. The fruit of the Spirit—the character of Christ being formed in us—needs to grow from the inside; it cannot be worn as an overall to cover our failings.

Perhaps you and your fellowship manage to avoid these problems—Alleluia! However, we can all benefit from studying the insidious way drivenness can creep into the life of a church. Part of this process will be to examine how our individual needs are being met. We *all* have needs—that's part of being human! I often have to reassure people: 'It's not a sin to be needy.' Humanity and human need both existed before the Fall although, as a consequence of the Fall, the range of human neediness expanded dramatically. As we know only too well, some of the ways in which we choose to *meet* our needs are sinful, but that does not mean that neediness is itself sinful.

Are we willing to admit to having needs? If so, are we meeting them in the ways God intended? We may not see ourselves as addicted to anything, but if we are using busyness and being needed, relationships, leadership authority or other aspects of church to meet needs which God never intended them to meet, we are on a dangerous route.

Let's take our courage in both hands and press on to see how the features associated with addiction can manifest themselves among God's people.

# Self-esteem problems

Some Christians find the whole concept of self-esteem (also called self-worth, self-regard) rather disturbing. In fact, some speak as if having a 'self' is itself sinful. Psychologically speaking, my 'self' is my sense of my own existence. To recognize that I have a 'self' does not mean that I am automatically 'selfish'. I do need to watch my attitude to my 'self', but it is not God's plan that I try to annihilate it, in order to have no self at all, as some seem to believe. The biblical picture is that we are to 'put off' the old self and *put on the new self*, 'created to be like God in true righteousness and holiness' (Ephesians 4:22–24).

## *Self-denial*

Christian teaching about self-denial has also caused considerable misunderstanding. Self-denial is not about denying our self-worth; it is about choosing to go against our self-*will*. (It's difficult to deny our self-will if we're not conscious of having a self—or a will.) Yes, we are exhorted to put to death all that belongs to our 'earthly nature' (Colossians 3:5). Self-denial is turning away from the old self which we have 'put off', in order that the new self, 'which is being renewed in knowledge in the image of its Creator' (Colossians 3:10) may more effectively flourish, growing and developing into the full creator-made identity which God purposed. Paul tells us to count ourselves dead to sin (Romans 6:11) but does not stop there: we are to count ourselves 'alive to God in Christ Jesus' (same verse). Teaching which exalts self-annihilation as the ultimate form of self-denial is not biblical. Self-denial is primarily about choosing to go God's way rather than our own. Note also that self-denial is a choice, and a choice we can make only for ourselves; forcing such a 'choice' on someone else is abusive, however well-intentioned.

## *God's workmanship*

For the Christian, thinking about self-worth will include choosing to take God's view of ourselves. Ephesians 2:10 says that 'we are God's workmanship', and, in Psalm 139 (Psalm 139:13–14),

David praises God for his wonderful works, among which he includes himself!

Some Christians are nervous about discussing their self-worth; they seem to fear that thinking of themselves at all risks thinking of themselves too highly. Romans 12:3 says: 'Do not think of yourself more highly than you ought', but then says that we are to think of ourselves 'with sober judgment'. The chapter goes on to emphasize that we all belong to the body of Christ, within which—by God's design—we have different gifts and functions. This theme is taken up in 1 Corinthians 12, where it is made clear that 'different' does not mean more or less valuable. Those who do not have a true sense of their own worth will find it very difficult to function within the body of Christ as God intended them to do. They'll prefer to divert their energy into trying to be like someone they admire, rather than seeking God's purposes for themselves and the unique gifting he has for them. Some may opt out altogether, telling themselves they're not worthy of belonging to the body of Christ. What a waste!

Are we comfortable with these ideas, or do we see the notion of self-worth as the beginning of the slippery slope towards pride and self-satisfaction? Whatever our comfort level, the fact remains: we are God's workmanship. From that fact may follow the realization that rubbishing his workmanship, far from being a sign of self-effacing modesty, could actually be offensive to God. When I choose to go on taking God's view of myself—a child of God, made by him and reborn into his family by grace—I am allowing truth to strengthen the fragile self-esteem which I developed as a child of fallible parents living in a broken and disordered world.

One of my favourite verses of scripture is 1 John 3:1, which says: 'How great is the love the Father has lavished on us, that we should be called children of God! And that is what we are!' If you struggle with feelings of worthlessness, make a conscious effort to allow this verse or one of the others I've just mentioned to colour your thoughts about yourself. What we say to ourselves about ourselves, hour after hour, day after day, has a powerful effect on our self-image. Try replacing any negative self-talk with truths from scripture—such as 'I am a much-loved child of God'—and see what happens.

## The root of workaholism

Different people show their lack of self-esteem in different ways. In his book *Honest to God? Becoming an Authentic Christian*, Bill Hybels, Pastor of the Willow Creek Community Church in Illinois, writes of how low self-esteem, and the personal insecurity which accompanies it, are often at the root of workaholism. While perpetuating the myth that they simply enjoy tremendous job satisfaction, workaholics can be risking everything in pursuit of the appreciation and approval of others which—they hope—will enable them to feel good about themselves.

Bill Hybels believes that experiencing God's love brings relief to those enmeshed in what he sees as a powerful addiction. He is frank about his own struggle with workaholism, and writes of the practical steps he took to ensure that it no longer had the opportunity to take over his life. These included setting limits to his working hours, and inviting a few close friends to check that he was keeping to them. At the time of making this decision he had a young family, and he determined to be at home with them four nights each week—not just at home bodily, with his thoughts elsewhere, but genuinely with his wife and family in every sense.

# Identity problems

Some Christian families and churches attach such importance to unanimity and orthodoxy that discussion and dialogue become impossible. To hold a different view on, for example, the ordination of women (or even on ordination itself!) may be simply unacceptable, however well-reasoned. To enjoy a different type of music may be regarded as evidence of demonic activity. Under such circumstances, it's very difficult to develop a full sense of personhood. Some will openly rebel, but others will sacrifice their identity and submit to the control for fear of what they might lose. Having no sense of their *individual* identity, they'll stick with the group which tells them who they are and what they think.

## *Crazy conforming*

Isn't this all rather far-fetched? Surely it couldn't happen in *our* church! Yet, following the traumatic break up of NOS, the cultic 'alternative worship' Nine O'Clock Service in Sheffield, some who had been involved spoke openly of how they had conformed to the likes and dislikes of their leader. This even extended to choosing to eat and drink what he was eating and drinking in a restaurant, knowing that if they expressed a different preference they risked being seen as making a power play. In his book *The Rise and Fall of the Nine O'Clock Service* Roland Howard gives examples, and writes: 'Hypersensitivity surrounded any behaviour that could be seen as a challenge to [the leader] or a statement of independence.'

No doubt, a few years earlier, members of NOS would have been sure it couldn't happen in their congregation. The signs of individual identity being annihilated can be very small to start with. Perhaps the best approach is to listen carefully to what people actually say when expressing an opinion or justifying a particular course of action. If someone says: 'Our house group (or church, or family) thinks this is the answer' or 'feels unhappy about this', it can be helpful to say: 'And what do *you* think (or feel)?'

So often, it's not a matter of who is right and who is wrong about the issue: it's a matter of encouraging individuals to think their own thoughts and to feel their own feelings. Just as choosing a different type of food in a restaurant should not be seen as a threat, having different views on the best way forward in evangelism, for example, should not be automatically seen as divisive. Often there is room for a variety of approaches—particularly in evangelism!—but if people are discouraged from making alternative suggestions the outcome will be monochrome rather than full colour.

## *Individuality*
## *need not be a threat to unity*

The picture of the body of Christ found in scripture clearly allows for individual identity as well as unity, distinctiveness as well as connectedness. Distinctiveness and individuality are not the same as individualism, in which the determination to plough one's own furrow regardless can be a threat to unity.

Every part of the body is connected to Christ the Head (see Colossians 1:18; 2:19). This gives unity of purpose without the different parts sacrificing their identity. But some churches still behave as if it would be better if every member were the same. In pursuit of 'unity', everyone is forced into a standard mould, regardless of their individuality and personal identity. Those who choose to submit to the standardization process may become fierce advocates of the unanimity and orthodoxy which they initially found so uncomfortable. Having struggled to accept it themselves, they may switch to energetically forcing it upon others. Any who show signs of wavering will be leaned on to be more sensible. Those who dare to break ranks will be seen as betrayers. They may even be called 'Judas'.

## *The dangers of unquestioning obedience*

In her book *For Your Own Good: The roots of violence in childrearing*, the psychoanalyst Alice Miller writes of the poisonous effects of teaching children to discount their own thoughts and feelings and to do as they are told—regardless. Her views echo my own concerns about churches which appear to value orthodoxy above all else. I believe that this approach can produce Christians who are more concerned to say and do the approved thing than to seek the Lord's face and be the people he intended them to be.

Miller's book was originally published in German, and she writes disturbingly of the parenting style which was the norm when Adolf Hitler and his contemporaries were in their formative years. There is little doubt in my mind that the emphasis on unquestioning obedience was a key feature in the upbringing of those who went on to commit multiple atrocities without apparent guilt—because they were obeying orders.

Children learn to say 'No' at a very early age. Parents find this very irritating! Why couldn't they learn to say 'Yes' first, instead of 'No'? Parents need to encourage children to say 'Yes' to a varied diet, bedtime, wearing a coat in freezing weather, standing still on railway platforms when the train is approaching, and so on. But adults who continually override a child's 'No', whether or not it is necessary to do so, will leave the child with little or no sense of its own autonomy and vulnerable to abuse by others. In the same way, churches which adopt a rigid, highly parental style of leadership will stunt their members' growth towards the sort of individual maturity which God intends, and which is a recurring theme in the apostle Paul's letters to churches and their leaders.

## Unhealthy passivity

Those who have not acquired a sense of their own competence may express it in a religious way by saying that they are trusting everything to God when in reality they are abdicating all responsibility and becoming passive. Christians need to *choose* to follow God's way, and to *choose* to trust him. These are active choices, involving committing our will in a particular direction and holding it there. They are not to be confused with the Christian equivalent of the ostrich position: head in the clouds instead of the sand, opting out and calling it 'faith'.

A further danger is that someone with little or no sense of their own competence may look to others to tell them what God's will for their life is, being sure that they couldn't possibly have any idea what it might be. They will place an unhealthy reliance on the discernment of others, and may come to the point where their mentors have to be consulted on every routine day-to-day decision. This will lay them open to abuse.

More generally, oppressive regimes can be surprisingly attractive to those who lack a sense of identity. They can offer structure and a form of security to people who otherwise feel all at sea. The opportunity to be 'somebody', albeit a lowly somebody—a tiny cog in a very large machine—can be warmly welcomed by those who fear that they are really 'nobodies'. Being controlled, or squeezed into a standard mould, is better than being ignored. They may be prepared to endure appalling abuse within the system, and still support it, because it is their only source of identity. They cannot afford to threaten its continuing existence for fear of what they might lose in the process. I believe that some Christian organizations might be described as abusive systems, and this subject is dealt with in more detail in chapter 6.

## *Difficulties with intimacy*

As mentioned in the previous chapter, problems with intimacy are very common. Perhaps I need to re-emphasize that, although the word 'intimacy' is often used as shorthand for sexual intercourse or other sexual behaviour, I am using the word in a much wider sense of getting closer to a person. This should of course be within appropriate boundaries, and should involve wisdom and due caution, but don't let's allow the misuses of intimacy to rob us of the benefits.

Churches can allow members to develop an *appearance* of intimacy, and even to feel that they are experiencing true intimacy —especially in fellowships where everyone is on first-name terms, with lots of hugging. It's possible for desolate loneliness to exist behind an appearance of all being well. There may be lots of chatting after a service or a meeting, but people may leave feeling they haven't been heard—and perhaps they haven't been! The chat itself can be the means to an end, its content only an accessory.

Some folk pride themselves on the number of people they know, when their knowing amounts to very little. They feel they've done something really worthwhile if they've cruised around after church greeting everyone, but the exchanges can be almost ritualistic: 'How are you?' 'Fine. How are *you*?' 'Fine.' We need to encourage each other to press on towards friendship and greater intimacy as part of encouraging growth towards maturity. It is also part of living out what it means to be the body of Christ, within which the parts are necessarily in meaningful communication.

# Physical and psychological problems

The physical and psychological problems associated with alcohol and other substance abuse are well known, although perhaps not as easy to recognize in the early stages as one might think. One of the questions we need to ask ourselves is this: are those whose eyes are bleary from late-night Christian meetings really that much healthier? Are those whose headaches or dodgy digestive systems are due to the pace and pressure of church life, or their punishing schedule of good works—but who keep on going back for more—really so much more laudable?

## 'Burn-out'

Burn-out is now a recognized condition among Christian leaders; not all cases are due to drivenness or addiction, but we do well to examine it in this context. Peter Meadows wrote of his own experience of burn-out:

> For several months I had been waking up exhausted, struggling through the day bowed down by a weariness of body, mind and spirit. All ability to concentrate had gone. My nerves were on edge. I would have given anything for someone to put a volume control on the Rice Krispies. Time at my desk often involved little more than rearranging the piles of paper. As someone who had previously drawn from a bottomless well of boundless energy, it was a shock to be sent home from a major Christian conference, where I was due to lead and speak, to take a complete rest. As one of the conference team assessed eloquently afterwards, 'Your lights were on but there was nobody home!' As I began my recuperation and recovery, a consultant psychiatrist told me, 'You are not going to die. It is just that you have been running too close to the edge for far too long.'

> Peter Meadows, *Pressure Points*

A friend of mine who is in church leadership fell asleep at the wheel of his car whilst crossing a bridge, high above a river. He survived, regaining consciousness in hospital. Is the workaholic pace of church life such that we are putting our leaders and our members at risk through such accidents?

## Confronting unacceptable behaviour

Christians are not exempt from the psychological problems which can accompany all addictions, including driven religion. However, within the church we usually bend over backwards to avoid noticing—let alone confronting—such signs as swinging moods and irritability with outbursts of temper. We reason that it is more charitable—even 'Christian'—to turn a blind eye and hope that it will pass. I am aware of people in different churches whose uncontrolled outbursts have damaged and undermined others. In spite of this, they have been allowed to continue to take pastoral responsibility for house groups or similar groups over a period of *years*.

It has been explained to me that the responsibility will act as an incentive to change. Drawing attention to their unacceptable behaviour is considered inadvisable, lest it discourage them. What about all the others who are being discouraged in the process! Looking in as an outsider, it has seemed to me that the church leaders were allowing the responsibility to continue, against their better judgment, because they feared the inevitable outburst if they dared to act. The word cowardice springs to mind.

The opposite reaction of marginalizing someone who becomes difficult to deal with is equally unhelpful. If someone's behaviour is unacceptable, for whatever reason, it's important to confront the behaviour without rejecting the person. In the heat of the confrontation they are likely to *feel* rejected, but if brothers and sisters in Christ are willing to remain alongside, they may be more open to a continuing relationship when they've cooled down. They may even be willing to risk going deeper and examining the roots of their problems.

Both allowing folk to continue unchallenged, *and* putting them beyond the pale with no way back, effectively denies the life-changing redemptive power of the gospel. How many churches and Christian organizations are hamstrung in their ministries by the knock-on effects? Gifted people are lost to Christian fellowship or service because they can no longer take the undermining. Other gifted individuals are lost by being effectively excommunicated rather than challenged to change.

## Assessing 'impaired judgment'

Christians are not exempt from the impaired judgment associated with drivenness. This may cause immense difficulties in church life, especially among the leadership. Those concerned need careful confronting in love, after seeking the Lord at some length, and perhaps also checking out with a trusted friend that an assessment of impaired judgment is not being brought when it is simply a matter of holding a different view. Some of what passes for 'speaking the truth in love' (Ephesians 4:15) in church life is more about voicing opinions and hurts than about truth, and is self-righteous rather than loving. Conversely, some 'forgiveness' is a manoeuvre to sidestep painful issues—the Christian equivalent of kissing and making up while keeping your fingers crossed behind your back.

## Denial

It is an unpalatable fact that Christians can practise denial as part of an addiction-driven lifestyle. It can be manifested as a jokey or patronizing attitude towards anyone who starts writing or talking about process addictions in the church! 'I'm addicted to breathing,' said Charles, as I was teaching at a training day for counsellors. Charles is a workaholic. He found the idea that any of the teaching might apply to him very threatening, so he muttered away, distracting those who were sitting near him.

Gerald was a lifelong smoker. A few seconds after the close of every service, he would be out of the church door and into the car park for a quick cigarette, before returning to the building to be sociable. I had observed this, but had not felt that it was appropriate to comment. However, one day Gerald was holding forth about a group of street lads who had taken to attending our evening service. The paraphernalia of 'church' were completely foreign to them, but they kept coming, in spite of the horrified looks of some church members who seemed to believe that they were in danger of getting mugged in church. About halfway through each service, the group used to troop out to the car park for a smoking break. They then filed back into the church for the rest of the service. Gerald was complaining about their smoking break, so I asked him whether shooting out the instant a service had finished was really so different. Gerald was very taken aback, and told me that I was being impertinent. He clearly did not wish to proceed with the discussion, so I left it. One of the features of denial is this: addictions are what *other* people have!

## What is 'normal'?

The practice of redefining normal should be a cause of considerable concern to us all. Some Christians hold that pursuing church activities at anything less than a workaholic pace is backsliding in the Christian life. By the same token, they may also regard the consequences, such as family breakdown, ill health or burn-out, as evidence of satanic attack on the lives of key Christian workers.

Is it not true that, as far as some Christian workers and ministries are concerned, Satan only needs to stand by and let things run their course? If key workers are seeking to dull their personal pain through driven behaviour, rather than pursuing wholeness in Christ, any Christian ministry will run into all sorts of difficulties. Through the effect on the family lives of workers the next generation will pick up the diseased attitudes and behaviours. It's like the story of *The Emperor's New Clothes*: no one dares to comment on how strange it is that everyone is pretending not to notice the odd behaviour of a leader. Anyone from outside who joins will have to choose between going along with the craziness or being the odd one out—neither of which makes for good mental and spiritual health.

When I was young I was taught a prayer at school which spoke of the Lord's service as 'perfect freedom'. Regrettably, many people's experience is of something more akin to bondage. As individuals and churches, we need to turn our faces resolutely towards the truth, and ask: how free are we, really? Are we daily encountering the truth himself, and continuing to be set free, or are we hedging ourselves about with little lies, and bigger lies, and colluding with corporate deception. Are we intermingling darkness with light in a vain attempt to make it all come right?

'God is light; in him there is no darkness at all. If we claim to have fellowship with him yet walk in the darkness, we lie...' (1 John 1:5–6). The only answer is to face both the truth about our situation and the truth himself, Jesus. 'If we confess our sins, he is faithful and just and will forgive us our sins and purify us from all unrighteousness... we have one who speaks to the Father in our defence—Jesus Christ, the Righteous One. He is the atoning sacrifice for our sins...' (1 John 1:9; 2:1–2).

# Spiritual bankruptcy

When drivenness, addiction or an obsession of any sort takes hold, commitment to Christ—previously fundamental to the person's whole outlook on life—may appear to count for nothing. The same applies to marriage vows and other promises which were intended to be kept when they were made.

## Christians sometimes lie

Sadly, some will swear that black is white. Some will even go as far as to invoke God as their witness. This is very difficult for those around them, because there is a reluctance to accept that someone who is known as a Christian is also a liar (maybe even a compulsive liar). Whilst 'love covers over a multitude of sins' (1 Peter 4:8), and pouncing immediately on every possible inaccuracy can only be destructive within a relationship or a fellowship, choosing not to confront *recurring lying* does no one any good. It provides a large foothold for the Evil One in the lives of *all* those involved.

More often than not, unless lying is confronted it eventually pressurizes others into behaviour which they later regret. They may simply maintain an uneasy silence when they know they should have spoken up. They may have to put it all down to a misunderstanding, when they understand all too well what has been happening. They may even find themselves bending the truth, in order not to contradict what has already been said or done. It certainly fails to provide motivation for the person who is lying to seek the pastoral help and life-changing security in Christ which they so greatly need. Confronting recurring lying is risky; passing by on the other side is always the attractive option.

## 'Respectable' addictions are no exception

In her book *Working Ourselves to Death*, Diane Fassel underlines the unpalatable truth that morality is a daily casualty of all addictions, even the so-called respectable ones like workaholism. When an addiction is being relentlessly pursued, nothing else seems to matter—and I do mean *nothing else*.

I cannot stress this too highly: Christians who use good works or religion addictively are on the road to spiritual bankruptcy just as surely as any other addict. In addition, using religious practices or activities (or work, or busyness, or anything) to suppress unpalatable inner realities can lead to a *fear of being found out*. This can lead to further dissembling as well as much anxiety.

There is little to be gained by scolding or lecturing the person concerned about neglecting relationships, breaking promises, double standards and so on. They've probably heard it all before anyway. They need to be encouraged to come out of denial and to look reality in the face with their *own eyes*, rather than always seeing the problem through the eyes of others. This may require skilled help. They can then take a long, hard look at where the pain is coming from—the pain that is driving them to pursue such a destructive form of anaesthesia. Then perhaps the inner realities can be dealt with in the way that God intends. For every single one of us, the only way forward is the same: facing the truth about ourselves, seeing things God's way, and choosing to follow his path to real cleansing and healing—rather than putting all our energies into keeping up appearances, while dying inside.

# What did Jesus do and say?

Many of the issues we've been covering seem to be modern-day problems, but if we look closely I think we'll find that most of them, although superficially different, are nothing new. Throughout the rest of the book we'll be seeking to apply the scriptures to the areas already raised. Let's begin by examining how Jesus dealt with the issue of religion.

## *Empty religion*

There *were* true God-fearing men among the religious leaders of Jesus' day, but Jesus clearly saw that many of them were not the spiritual giants they claimed to be. He spoke forcefully on the subject of outward spiritual expertise which cloaked spiritual poverty —or worse! He called the Pharisees 'whitewashed tombs, which look beautiful on the outside but on the inside are full of dead men's bones and everything unclean' (Matthew 23:27). And God's abhorrence of their empty but poisonous type of religion is stated in no uncertain terms in the Old Testament too.

When Jesus spoke out, he did so against the backdrop of a succession of prophets who had said remarkably similar things in their day. When Jesus said, 'These people come near to me with their mouth and honour me with their lips, but their hearts are far from me. Their worship of me is made up only of rules taught by men,' he was quoting Isaiah 29:13. (Jesus refers to this quote in Matthew 15:8 and Mark 7:6.) Jeremiah expresses similar thoughts when he says to God (Jeremiah 12:2), 'You are always on their lips but far from their hearts.'

Earlier in Matthew's Gospel (Matthew 12:7) Jesus had quoted what God had said through the prophet Hosea (Hosea 6:6): 'For I desire mercy, not sacrifice, and acknowledgment of God rather than burnt offerings.' People had become experts at working the system, and found it relatively easy to do the rituals God had asked them to follow—relatively easy, that is, compared with *being the people he intended them to be*. The sacrifices and burnt offerings which were intended to be *part* of the structure of their relationship with God had become the centre-piece, the be-all and end-all. In the absence of an integrated spirituality—lives incorporating heart attitudes of worship and sacrifice—they were just going through the motions, and as far as God was concerned their religion *stank*. 'I hate, I despise your religious feasts; I cannot stand your assemblies... Away with the noise of your songs!' (Amos 5:21, 23) 'Your burnt offerings are not acceptable; your sacrifices do not please me' (Jeremiah 6:20). 'Stop bringing meaningless offerings! Your incense is detestable to me... Your New Moon festivals and your appointed feasts my soul hates' (Isaiah 1:13–14). This subject is explored further in Study 2, 'What's wrong with religion?' at the end of the book.

## A challenge

By healing on the Sabbath, Jesus challenged the attitudes of those whose obsessional observance of the law blinded them to the needs of people suffering right in front of them. During his time on earth he turned upside-down much of the thinking of his contemporaries concerning what was—or was not—true religion. The Son of God spoke with *authority* about what was acceptable. In stark contrast to those who loved fine-tuning the system of complicated rules and regulations, he really knew what God required.

Are we willing to allow him to challenge *our* blind spots? Is it possible that we've been trying to find our security in following the letter of the law, in agreeing with powerful people, or in loyalty to a particular way of doing things? Have we tried to find significance by caring, leading, worshipping and saying 'Yes' to everything until we drop—in doing, rather than being? Have we been so busy over-dosing on religion that we have neglected the riches of God's grace?

I firmly believe that God delights to lead towards wholeness all who are willing to bring their neediness to him. This will take courage, patience, time, and probably also a group of supportive friends to provide long-term back-up and a degree of accountability during the process. The gospel is only good news if we allow it to impact our real needs—to meet us where we are and move us on. If we use religious activities and church commitments as accessories in the window-dressing of impoverished lives, they can be very bad news indeed.

## Focus point

**'What would I be doing if I weren't...?'**

Is it possible that you have a tendency to retreat into church or other activities to blot out pain or difficulties closer to home?

Ask those closest to you: **'What is the cost to you of what I do in and for the church?'**

Listen carefully and patiently to their answers, however unjust you feel they may be. Reflect on what has been said. Reflect on the feelings this has aroused.

Take your thoughts and feelings to the Lord, and ask him to give insight and wisdom.

*The Message* translates 1 Thessalonians 4:1 as follows: 'One final word, friends. We ask you—*urge* is more like it—that you keep on doing what we told you to do to please God, not in a dogged religious plod, but in a living, spirited dance.'

Would you describe your life as more plod than dance, or vice versa? Is it possible that your dance has become more frenzied than spirited?

Ask God how he sees it.

# Keeping up appearances

### 1 Samuel 16:7

*The Lord does not look at the things man looks at. Man looks at the outward appearance, but the Lord looks at the heart.*

### Hebrews 4:13

*Nothing in all creation is hidden from God's sight. Everything is uncovered and laid bare before the eyes of him to whom we must give account.*

How do you respond to these verses of scripture? Do they make you feel nervous...? Or do they bring the relief that comes from knowing that you don't have to pretend to God?

The BBC TV character Mrs Hyacinth Bucket (pronounced 'Bouquet') sums up that way of life which is founded upon 'Keeping Up Appearances'. Her life is centred around the importance of saying and doing the right thing, doing the right thing in the right way, and making sure that the right people know all about it. When for one reason or another it's impossible to do the right thing, she devises an elaborate charade designed to make everyone else believe that she *has* done it, often involving her beleaguered husband in her relentless pursuit of social perfection.

## Appearances connected to reality

Everyone can see the folly of Mrs Bucket's existence, but does that mean that appearances are unimportant? Certainly not! Jesus in the Sermon on the Mount encouraged his followers with the words: '…let your light shine before men, that they may see your good deeds and praise your Father in heaven' (Matthew 5:16). In his parting words to them in the upper room, he said: 'By this all men will know that you are my disciples, if you love one another' (John 13:35). Appearances are part of our calling to communicate the gospel to those around us, and to bring glory to God. But what is seen is only valid if it's a true representation of an inner reality.

## *Heart attitudes bear fruit—good or bad*

If we are very appearance-orientated, our hearts will clamour for all that looks good, neglecting to welcome that which really is good. Instead of allowing our hearts to be soil in which the fruit of the Spirit may grow, we'll be filling them with the spiritual equivalent of astroturf and imitation pot plants. This will smother any tiny shoots of true spiritual growth, and our hearts will be stony ground rather than fertile soil.

Jesus castigates the Pharisees in Matthew 23 for their pursuit of outward correctness in all religious practices. The aspects of the law relating to attitudes of heart and mind are described by Jesus as 'more important' (Matthew 23:23). In any case, says Jesus, sooner or later a person's true character will be seen in the fruit his life brings: 'No good tree bears bad fruit, nor does a bad tree bear good fruit… The good man brings good things out of the good stored up in his heart, and the evil man brings evil things out of the evil stored up in his heart. For out of the overflow of his heart his mouth speaks' (Luke 6:43, 45).

In Matthew 6:1 Jesus says: 'Be careful not to do your "acts of righteousness" before men, to be seen by them.' It's easy to hurry past this verse as if it only applied to someone else. It doesn't. Jesus goes on to warn against behaving like the hypocrites, whom Eugene Peterson in *The Message* calls 'play-actors'. (Our English word hypocrite is derived from the Greek word *hupokrites*, which means 'one who plays a part'.) Their charitable giving, prayer and fasting were done in public for maximum effect. Jesus' words seem to imply that these worthy things done with an eye to public honour were of no value at all in God's sight. We may not feel it appropriate to dignify our Christian service with the phrase 'acts of righteousness', but if we're doing whatever it is we're doing with one eye on how many points we'll be earning in people's eyes, we need to come in repentance to receive cleansing from God.

## The age of the image

We live in a world which emphasizes appearances. Image consultancy is a multi-million pound business. Training courses for executives teach them how to create the right impression, and how to ensure that they reinforce their words with their body-language so that any uncertainties they may have about their product or promised delivery dates aren't communicated to clients.

It's easy for the church to get sucked into the image business. I'm all for Christians updating their publicity production methods so that what comes out looks like something someone might want to read, rather than a 1960s printer's reject. I am convinced that the church needs to move with the times, and use modern methods of communication, but it's not OK to doctor the message to make the church sound more appealing than it really is. If what happens in church is so boring and irrelevant that even the faithful few who gather are secretly wishing they didn't have to, reformatting the publicity designed to encourage new members isn't going to help. If those who gather are happy as they are and resent the intrusion of newcomers, putting up attractive posters and making a 'welcome pack' isn't the answer.

The world increasingly takes the view that if things aren't humming along nicely a change of image is called for. We need to make sure that we're not taken in—that we don't try to smarten things up on the outside when the only answer is radical change on the inside.

# Prevention is better than cure

As a child, were you forced to say 'Sorry', even if you weren't? I've never felt it right to force my own children to go through the motions of saying 'Sorry' when they were clearly feeling something very different, because it could teach them that it doesn't matter if you're seething inside, as long as you appear penitent on the outside. How can we explain to children about saying sorry to

God, meaning coming in confession and repentance when we have sinned, if we've taught them that saying sorry is an empty process of mouthing the right words?

I was talking this through with a friend called Molly, and she told me that she and her husband had encouraged their children only to say sorry if they meant it, and had explained to them that 'Sorry is something you only say if you're not going to do it again'.

## Not teaching children to pretend

As a parent I understand the importance of teaching children to be well-mannered and to have consideration for others. This will include instructing them that they are not to repeat certain actions, whether or not they are sorry, and that some things have to be done whether or not they feel like it. It will also include dissuading them from speaking out their every thought about every person and situation they encounter. I remember being embarrassed when pushing one of my sons up the road in his pushchair. We passed a man who was working on his car. A little voice piped up: 'That man's got *very* dirty hands!' The man didn't see the funny side of it. I would have preferred my son to keep his thoughts to himself on this occasion!

Encouraging children to have respect for the feelings and privacy of others is very different from telling them to call 'dirty' 'clean', or in some other way to collude in misrepresenting reality. We've probably all heard a variation of the story of a family entertaining visitors to lunch. A young child is being encouraged to say grace before the meal. 'Just say what Daddy says,' urges her mother. 'You know, "O Lord…".' 'O Lord, why did we invite those dreadful people to lunch?' prays the child, innocently.

Children of alcoholic parents speedily learn about lying in order to keep up appearances. They may be directed to lie about what has happened to their dinner money (spent on drink) or the reason for their absence from school (parent too hung over to drive them there). They may also be drawn into lying to the wider family, to an employer, to the rent man, and so on. They lie because they are told to, but also because they know that their lives will be made even more intolerable if they don't.

Sadly, some children in Christian families are pressurized into saying things they know are not true in order to foster an image of family life which is far from reality. They may also feel pressurized *not* to say things which they know *are* true, for fear of letting the side down. They've learned that it's the window display that counts.

## *Putting on religion rather than growing faith*

Many children are dragged unwillingly to church week after week. They are forced to participate in activities whether or not their heart is in them. This is a difficult issue. All children go through phases of having likes and dislikes, and wanting to go somewhere (for example, swimming or horse-riding) one week and joining a club with great enthusiasm, only to feel differently in a week or two's time. Parents need to encourage children to press on through the ups and downs, but they also need to be willing to hear what their children are saying—or to sense what they would be saying if they didn't fear a volcanic reaction!

Our children went hot and cold about church over many years. Our solution was to insist that they came with us on Sunday mornings while they were too young to stay at home on their own, but we didn't force them to participate if they were unwilling to do so. As they grew older we allowed them to exercise their own choice; we always asked them if they were coming, and tried not to frown if they said 'No.'

It's possible to argue that children who are allowed to opt out of church will miss out on hearing the gospel there, and that's true. But it's probably also true that what goes on at home will be just as important (if not more so) in forming their attitudes than an hour or two in church or Sunday School each week. Seeing the scriptures being applied in family relationships and lifestyle choices (or not applied, as the case may be) will be very influential.

It's easy to overvalue the achievement of getting a full family turnout at church every week. I do not underestimate the pressure that there is on church leaders to 'play Happy Families' and arrive with a full complement of scrubbed, smiling offspring with conventional haircuts and clothes. But if a young person in the process of establishing their identity prefers to spend Sunday at another church, or in bed, or chooses to turn up with purple hair and an earring, is that really such a disaster?

Some children of committed Christians seem to manage to 'play the game', attending church and saying and doing the right things throughout their teens, and then kick over the traces in a big way when they leave home. On balance, it's much better to allow them the freedom to exercise their own choices (within age-appropriate boundaries) while they are still living with their parents. This includes allowing *them* to decide what they believe, and to discuss their views outside the family if they wish to do so, without fear of accusations of letting the side down if they choose to say that they do not share their parents' faith. It's vital that parents do not sacrifice their children's identity or integrity on the altar of appearances.

# Being real with God and others

In November 1995 Ann Warren (freelance writer, broadcaster and pastoral counsellor) contributed a short series to the multi-author *Alive to God* Bible Reading Notes, published by Scripture Union. It was entitled 'Being real with God', and tackled some of the destructive effects of *not* being real with God, pointing out the impact this makes not just on our own lives but on the lives of others. On one of the days she shared how, after she had begun counsellor training, she became aware of a lack of reality in the Bible study group she led. Everything seemed stuck on a superficial level. There was much discussion of the meaning of passages, but little obvious fruit in people's lives. After Ann eventually managed to express how difficult she found all this, and after people had recovered from the shock, others began to tell of similar feelings, sharing needs and questions which they had not dared to voice. Ann's willingness to be honest was the catalyst for the development of the group, which benefited everyone.

## *Masks and games*

In *Pathways of Prayer*, broadcaster, author and theologian Angela Tilby is quoted as saying:

> *I have always felt a bit of a struggle within Christian culture. We are encouraged to be rather self-sufficient and to cultivate an image that is untroubled, unangry, that doesn't hate, that doesn't ever despair. And if we do hate or are angry or despair, we do it very privately and don't let it be known or seen. I think there is something not terribly healthy about living in that sort of armour, and we've all been encouraged to do it, I think. It's partly a sort of English thing. But it's a sort of Christian thing as well.*

> Pathways of Prayer, edited by Graham Dow

When we become Christians we need to be willing to examine the way we behave. Our culture may regard what we do and say (or what we refrain from saying) as normal and acceptable—even laudable—but does the Bible take a different view?

Writing in 2 Corinthians 4:2 about his policy on preaching the gospel, Paul advocated transparency, declaring: 'We refuse to wear masks and play games' (*The Message*). Later in the chapter (same version, verse 16) he assures everyone that 'even though on the outside it often looks like things are falling apart on us, on the inside, where God is making new life, not a day goes by without his unfolding grace.' Our approach can be just the opposite! Have you ever caught yourself pouring a lot of effort into putting on a good show while dying inside?

For some folk, keeping up appearances is more than an acquired habit; it's not a 'game' they can choose to stop playing. They feel that their whole being—their very existence—is under threat: if people found out what they were really like they would be rejected, humiliated, or worse. They can be helped by being in day-to-day contact with people who nurture and encourage them, and who practise openness in their own lives—sharing their sorrows as well as joys, and being real about their own failings in a healthy rather than a morbid way. Knowing God's unconditional love and acceptance, and receiving it from others, will contribute to their healing, but they may also require skilled help in coming to understand why they have such a strong need to hide behind a façade. However the help comes, God's people will need to provide lots of encouragement along the way. But it's important to be aware that it can be a mistake to try to build someone like this up with lots of encouraging words but with no reference to the very real problem that we all have: the problem of sin.

## *Being real about sin*

Since the Garden of Eden we have feared exposure. When we sin, our immediate reaction is so often to cover it over, hoping that no one saw—and that, if they did see, they won't tell. Gerald Coates writes provocatively: 'We need to nurture churches where people are allowed to be real and where people are allowed to sin.' He goes on to explain: 'That does not mean encouraged to sin, or that there should be churches that condone sin. But if we build churches which do not allow people to sin, they have to cover up. Instead of the church becoming a focus of reality, openness and vulnerability, it becomes the arena for its own myths, fantasies and cover-ups' (Gerald Coates, *Nonreligious Christianity*).

Invited to preach on the subject of forgiveness, I began with the bad news that every preacher heard so far that year was a sinner, and that the preacher that morning was no exception. I went on to reveal that, after the church had waited many months for a new rector, the appointing panel had given the job to a sinner. There was a nervous silence. *What* did I know? *How* did I know?

I asked the congregation to turn to Romans 3:23 which tells us that 'all have sinned'. The good news which followed was that the rector and I were forgiven sinners. And there was even better news too! The same forgiveness is available to everyone else. (The book of Romans goes on to explain that we are justified freely by grace and details the whole process.)

The nervousness which accompanied my revelation that the new rector was a sinner took me rather by surprise. (He was sitting not far away and nodding!) Since his arrival four months previously, Chris had been at pains to point out that he was not perfect, and that he didn't see himself as the answer to everyone's needs. Perhaps some had received these comments as evidence of touching modesty, and disregarded them! He'd been open about his failings, but had he been heard? Was it perhaps too threatening to accept that the new wonder-guy might not merely fall a little short but from time to time actually... (sshhh, not too loud) sin? Might his openness be pressing us gently to confront our own failings? Might we even have to take a closer look and see if there were any… (sshhh) sins to be dealt with?

## Asking God's forgiveness

Why do we behave like this when the scriptures clearly describe us as sinners? Why do we opt for living behind a façade, erecting whitewashed tombstones over the dark secrets in our lives? Why do we favour keeping the dirty washing (everyone else's as well as our own) well-hidden, fermenting in the laundry basket? Is there nothing to be said for getting it out and dealing with it in the way God provides?

As an Anglican church, we use a form of confession in our main services. Week by week we appear to acknowledge before God that we have sinned and need his forgiveness, but are we seeing this as a quaint old Anglican custom rather than a true representation of our state? 'Forgive us our sins,' says the Lord's Prayer. Jesus gave it to his disciples (Luke 11:2–4) as an example of how to pray, and it's still widely used. But how often do we ask for our sins to be forgiven without being willing to own what's coming from our lips?

Jesus told a story about two men. One of them, a tax collector, recognized his need for forgiveness, asked God for it, and went home having been made right with God. The other didn't.

> 'Two men went up to the Temple to pray, one a Pharisee, the other a tax man. The Pharisee posed and prayed like this: "Oh, God, I thank you that I am not like other people—robbers, crooks, adulterers, or, heaven forbid, like this tax man. I fast twice a week and tithe on all my income."
>
> 'Meanwhile the tax man, slumped in the shadows, his face in his hands, not daring to look up, said, "God, give mercy. Forgive me, a sinner."'
>
> Jesus commented, 'This tax man, not the other, went home made right with God. If you walk around with your nose in the air, you're going to end up flat on your face, but if you're content to be simply yourself, you will become more than yourself.'
>
> (Luke 18:10–14, *The Message*)

Trying to keep up an appearance of sinlessness is not only point-less (we're unlikely to be able to fool more than some of the people some of the time), it actually bars the way to our becoming all that God wants us to be. In addition, it creates a climate in which Christians are more concerned about creating a good impression than about being forgiven. Pause for a moment and think about this—it's dynamite! Given the choice between the complete for-giveness and cleansing which God offers, and the inadequate cos-metic job we try to do for ourselves, there should be no contest! What's the problem?

## Acknowledging our sin

The Psalms include many expressions of the various writers' awareness of how their sin distanced them from God. Psalm 51 was written by King David after the prophet Nathan had con-fronted him with his adultery with Bathsheba. Adultery resulted in pregnancy, and eventually led to what amounted to murder to cover his tracks (see 2 Samuel 11 and 12 for the full story). David pleads for God's mercy. But we need to note that he also ac-knowledges that it can't all be put right merely by going through a religious formality.

> *You do not delight in sacrifice, or I would bring it;*
> *you do not take pleasure in burnt offerings.*
> *The sacrifices of God are a broken spirit;*
> *a broken and contrite heart,*
> *O God, you will not despise.*
>
> (Psalm 51:16–17)

If we ask for God's forgiveness without any intention of turning away from the sin we're confessing, we are unrepentant. David recognized that God required genuine repentance, not just a going through of the religious motions associated with repentance. The same understanding is shown by the prophet Joel when he ex-horts God's people: 'Rend your heart and not your garments' (Joel 2:13). (For further study and reflection on 'Real sin, real grace, real forgiveness', see Study 3 at the end of the book.)

## Being a good witness...
## or protecting ourselves?

We may seek to justify deceiving unbelievers about what we are really like, on the grounds of not wanting to dishonour the Lord. But how does the Lord himself feel about having his name associated with such an ill-conceived public relations exercise? Has he not already made adequate provision for dealing with the consequences of our fallen nature—a provision that involves facing the truth, rather than concealment? I believe that keeping up appearances within the body of Christ is abhorrent to him, and is responsible for much of that body's emaciation.

Pearl and Robert had been sent overseas as missionaries from a large church in a country town. Their marriage was fraught with difficulties, and Pearl eventually returned to their home town in a state of considerable distress and shut herself away. The church continued to list the couple as missionaries overseas, and Pearl's presence in the town was not mentioned, even though members of the congregation knew that she had returned and were unhappy about the continuing deception. Eventually, of course, the painful truth had to be told. But, meanwhile, who had been protecting whom?

We are probably all aware that Christians sometimes disagree, even when everyone is trying hard to follow the Lord. When I left a Christian organization because I was unhappy about some things that were happening within it, the colleagues who remained decided to report in their next newsletter that I had left 'for personal reasons'. Fortunately, I heard about this before it was published, and they agreed to delete the phrase 'for personal reasons'. I was unhappy that they seemed to want to imply that my reasons for leaving were connected with matters outside the organization, when they knew that to be untrue. I found this a painful end to a difficult working relationship.

## Keeping the peace?

We are keen to create a good impression by appearing united and of one mind in the Lord's service. This can be taken to ridiculous extremes, such that any discussions are minefields, and honest disagreements are taboo. This is mistakenly called 'keeping the peace'. But peace is not the covering over of conflict.

Sometimes it's just a matter of people seeing things differently, but sometimes conflict is due to sin, and trying to gloss over it or sweep it under the carpet in the name of peace doesn't work with sin. We need to face the fact that when we choose not to confront the sin of others it may be because we don't want to lose their goodwill, or because we fear that they may retaliate. Might they perhaps turn the spotlight on our own failings? Our primary motive may be self-protection, however much we dress it up in more spiritual clothing.

## A storm in a teacup?

Jane, a minister's wife, was frequently battered by her husband, Colin. He had a preaching ministry which attracted visitors from far and wide. From time to time, as they got ready to go to church, Colin used to tell his wife to put on a dress with longer sleeves because the bruises he had inflicted were showing. He kept his image pristine. He was a success. Jane finally decided that she had no alternative but to leave him after he began to hit his twin sons. While making plans to escape, she continued to behave as if nothing was wrong, in order not to arouse her husband's suspicions. She did not want to be at risk of further violence if he found out that she planned to leave, and she feared that he might prevent her taking the children with her.

One afternoon, Jane and the children made their way to a safe house in another part of the country, taking very little in the way of clothes or possessions. When news of their departure leaked out, many people were sure that the tales of violence couldn't possibly be true. Years of careful impression management had done the trick. Colin had worked meticulously to control the impressions everyone received of himself as a person and of his family. Jane had feared the consequences of telling a different story. Colin continued in ministry. The church authorities chose to accept his version—that it was a storm in a teacup. They did encourage him to seek counselling, but he never really got the help he needed. The church was more interested in getting him back to work, and stabilizing the rocking boat, than in encouraging him to get to grips with his problems.

## A loyal wife?

Many a Christian woman has been exhorted to 'be a good, loyal and submissive wife' and to cover up or excuse her husband's violent behaviour. Wives of violent husbands are in any case slow to seek help, because they know the punishment that awaits them if they dare to step out of line. In addition, the teaching they have received over the years may have led them to believe that they should not confront their husbands. Some have been told that the exhortation to submit in order that their husbands be won over without a word (1 Peter 3:1) applies to their situation. In fact this verse was written specifically to wives whose husbands were unbelievers, and I'm sure it was never intended to be an argument for silently enduring any and every form of marital unpleasantness. The same advice is sometimes given to women whose husbands are unfaithful. A minister's wife who lets the cat out of the bag when her husband has committed adultery can be shunned for being disloyal, and accused of trying to destroy God's work!

Dr Peter Rutter, a psychotherapist, has written frankly of the corporate denial which is so often practised when clergy are found to have abused their position of trust. He reports that the clergy are often simply transferred. Elsewhere in the same book, Rutter writes: 'I could not locate a single published statistical study of sexual misconduct among clergymen. However, colleagues who are knowledgeable in this area believe that its incidence among male clergy exceeds the ten per cent estimate for male psychotherapists' (Peter Rutter, *Sex in the Forbidden Zone*).

## 'I can't believe it'

Rutter decided to write his book about what he came to call 'sex in the forbidden zone' after two episodes in his life radically changed his outlook and underlined the need for openness about the subject. The first was a 'near-sexual encounter with a woman patient' which forced him to acknowledge his own vulnerability. 'The second episode,' he writes, 'the disclosure that a psychiatrist who had been my mentor and role model had for years been engaged in sex with many of his women patients, shattered my naïveté so profoundly that I felt compelled to look as deeply as I could into this problem as a way of reshaping my sense of reality.'

He goes on to describe how, even when he came to believe that the accusations about his mentor were true, it took him years (yes, really—years!) to absorb that truth sufficiently to be able to act upon it, and to join others in voting to expel him from the professional association. Since then, his research has shown that it is not unusual for ethical men to take no action when they become aware of a colleague's sexual exploits breaking well-recognized professional codes.

It's now some years since my own world was turned upside-down by the discovery that a fellow Christian with leadership responsibilities was leading a double life. It was fortunate that I was not among those responsible for deciding how to proceed, because I experienced the paralysis which Rutter describes. I was emotionally in shock for several months. Yes, it is easier to minimize the problem—to pretend that, if it *did* happen… (and denial can come into play here such that, even with overwhelming evidence, we prefer to keep an element of doubt) if it *did* happen, it definitely won't happen again, so we can all put it behind us, and needn't take any action.

## Justice and mercy

Whilst working on this chapter, I received a tape cassette from an evangelist whose work we have supported over the years. After giving news of current prayer needs, he went on to share what was on his heart about the importance of embracing *both* 'loving mercy' *and* 'acting justly' (Micah 6:8). He shared how he had been sexually abused as a teenager by someone in a position of authority in a Christian ministry. He recognized the wrong which had been done to him, but did not see it as appropriate to make public accusations. He was eventually able to release forgiveness to the man and to move on. Some years later he heard how the same man had subsequently abused others, and realized that by being merciful yet not also 'acting justly' he had left the way open for this.

About two hundred years earlier the politician and philosopher Edmund Burke had written: 'The only thing necessary for the triumph of evil is for good men to do nothing.' Centuries before that, James had summarized at the end of a difficult chapter: 'Anyone, then, who knows the good he ought to do and doesn't do it, sins' (James 4:17).

What's the answer? Should the whole truth be told whatever the likely outcome? It would be simple to say 'Yes', but life is never simple, and in any case only God knows the whole truth. I believe part of the answer is that we must be open before the Lord, and scrupulously honest with ourselves. If we are able to recognize when our reluctance to let the whole truth be known is—at least in part—because of a desire to protect ourselves, we are less likely to get involved with lies dressed up as seeking to protect the Lord's name. Anyway, he can take care of himself!

# Holiness and perfection

I think that it was in the 1960s that toilet deodorizers were first available in this country. Before that, toilet products were marketed on their cleaning ability rather than on the impression they left behind. These days, supermarket shelves sport an array of products designed to make toilets smell of everything from roses to pine forests! In some cases, there's no suggestion that the purchaser's toilet will be any cleaner—simply that it will smell wonderful! A fragrance associated with cleanliness can give a false sense of security while the germs multiply unchecked. It can be tempting to adopt the same approach to dealing with spiritual issues.

## What is holiness?

Peter (1 Peter 1:16) quotes the book of Leviticus, in which God tells his people specifically on four occasions that they must be holy because he is holy. The Bible says, 'Be holy', not 'Act holy' or 'Appear holy'. But we find this holiness business very difficult, and may choose to settle for an appearance of holiness, which—we hope—will fool at least some of the people some of the time, and show God how hard we're trying.

There's a widespread misunderstanding about what holiness is. It's not actually a matter of looking pious, speaking in a certain way or doing religious acts; it's about being devoted to God. In the Old and New Testaments the words translated 'holy' carry with them the idea of being separated out, dedicated for a purpose. Once we have responded to the call of God upon our lives, we need to be willing participants in the on-going process of sanctification ('holy-making') which God, by his Holy Spirit, works in the lives of all his saints ('holy ones'). A life that is totally dedicated to God will include words and actions which reflect that dedication, but the outward signs are there only because of the inner devotion. An 'appearance of holiness' is a worthless and potentially dangerous counterfeit, which we parade before the world and the church at our peril.

## *Being perfect*

The King James Version of the Bible urges us to be perfect (for example: 2 Corinthians 13:11; 2 Timothy 3:17). The New International Version continues to translate Matthew 5:48 as: 'Be perfect, therefore, as your heavenly Father is perfect.' There is a problem: in our minds, the word 'perfect' is usually associated with something which is flawless, without blemish. But those who received the letters to churches which became our Epistles would have had very different mental images. The Greek word used in 2 Corinthians 13:11 is *katartizo*, which means 'made complete, fit for the job, or rightly ordered'. A different Greek word is used by Jesus in Matthew 5:48: *teleios* has to do with being finished, fulfilled, completed, accomplished, fully grown and mature.

Neither of these Greek words means 'without blemish'; the word for that is *amomos*. Peter uses *amomos* of Jesus (1 Peter 1:19) when he describes him as a 'lamb without blemish or defect', the one who redeemed us from our empty way of life by his precious blood (see also Hebrews 9:14).

We can be counted *amomos* (without blemish, without fault, blameless) in God's sight only because of what Jesus did on the cross. See, for example, Colossians 1:21–22: 'Once you were alienated from God and were enemies in your minds because of your evil behaviour. But now he has reconciled you by Christ's physical body through death to present you holy in his sight, without blemish and free from accusation.' (See also Jude 24.) Let us be quite clear about this: by determination and concentrated effort we cannot attain a state of blamelessness. But the recognition that we cannot make ourselves blameless is not a licence to sin while revelling in God's grace (see Romans 6:1–2; Paul had thought of that argument!) It is, or should be, an incentive to praise God for his mercy, to thank him for his grace, and to live lives which bear all the hallmarks of being set apart for God's use.

The scriptures encourage us to gratefully accept all that Jesus has done to take away our sin, making us blameless in God's sight. The scriptures also encourage us to accept the 'teaching, rebuking, correcting and training in righteousness' they bring, in order that we may be 'perfect' (AV), 'thoroughly equipped for every good work' (NIV) (2 Timothy 3:16–17).

## Grace and works

Some people would point to a number of apparent contradictions in scripture which they perceive because they misunderstand the differing functions of 'grace' and 'works'. For example, in Philippians 2:12 Paul exhorts the Philippian Christians to continue to work out their salvation. Down the centuries some Christians have allowed this verse to be a rod for their back, and they've rightly been criticized by other Christians for trying to do sufficient to earn or in some way merit their salvation. But Paul's point here is about our manner of life, the outworking of our salvation, not the basis for it. In verses 14 and 15 he goes on: 'Do everything without complaining or arguing, so that you may become blameless [*amemptos*—a related Greek word] and pure, children of God without fault [*amomos*] in a crooked and depraved generation…' Perhaps the key verse here is the one I've left out, which says: 'for it is God who works in you to will and to act according to his good purpose' (Philippians 2:13).

Just as we are saved for eternity by grace and not by works, yet are called to live lives which exemplify salvation and are worthy of our calling (Ephesians 4:1), so we achieve blamelessness by grace alone, yet are called to aim for nothing less than blamelessness in our lives. In addition, our love for God and our desire to draw close to him will surely motivate us to try to live our lives in ways which please him. That will mean taking Jesus, the only truly blameless one, as our example to follow. Blamelessness is the standard we are set, and we are to aim for it wholeheartedly—but without deceiving ourselves, imagining that one day we'll reach it by our own striving.

'Grace' does for us that which we are incapable of doing for ourselves: God, by grace, accepts the sacrifice of Christ as full payment of the penalty for our sin; by grace our relationship with our holy God is restored. 'Works' cannot pay the penalty, and are impotent when it comes to restoring our relationship with a holy God—we haven't a hope without grace. But our works, our lives, can *express* that restored relationship, and give us an opportunity to demonstrate what by grace we have become.

## *Truly clean, truly dedicated*

So, when we're encouraged by the scriptures to aim for holiness and perfection, we're not being told to do for ourselves what only Jesus can do for us. Neither are we being told to smarten up our spiritual acting. On the contrary! God is looking for real evidence of devotion to him, and an inner transformation which leaves us fit for his purposes. Are we in the process of becoming the complete, full-grown, mature men and women he plans for us to be?

# Focus point

**'Am I prepared to be real about my sin—and to receive real forgiveness? Or is my concern mainly to give an appearance of being OK?'**

Look up Romans 3:23 and 1 John 1:9, and read them in their context. Reflect on the difference between spring-cleaning and window-dressing.

**'Do I have one eye on what people are seeing when I'm worshipping and serving God?'**

Read Matthew 6:1–6, and ask God to show you how he sees things. If you become aware of sin, confess it to God and receive his forgiveness and cleansing.

If 'what people will think' is a major pressure in your life, ask God to show you where this is coming from.

If you have children of your own, or are in regular contact with children, reflect on what you have been teaching them by your attitudes to 'what people will think'.

# Keeping people happy

### Galatians 1:10

*Am I trying to please men? If I were still trying to please men,
I would not be a servant of Christ.*

### John 12:42—43

*Many even among the leaders believed in him. But... they would not
confess their faith for fear they would be put out of the synagogue; for
they loved praise from men more than praise from God.*

I was brought up to consider the effect my words and actions
would have on others, and I have encouraged my own children to
do the same. But I've also taught them that if someone is unhappy about something we've said or done, that doesn't automatically mean we were wrong to do or say it; we must avoid
making other people's approval the overriding factor in our lives.
Otherwise, as Paul observes above, we would not decide to serve
Christ! John's observation (above) that some of the leaders 'loved
praise from men more than praise from God' should serve as a
challenge to us all—especially if we are in leadership. Is there
something we'd dearly love to be doing if we weren't so afraid of
upsetting people?

## Approval-seeking leads to...

The desire not to upset people, the desire to keep them happy,
sounds innocent enough, and may even be presented as a charm-

ing Christian virtue. But in practice it can lead to lying and all sorts of deceitfulness, and result in loss of trust and broken fellowship. If we say what we think others want to hear, irrespective of the truth, and go along with their plans regardless of our concerns about their wisdom or legitimacy, how can this possibly be seen as a virtue?

Paul encouraged the Christians at Ephesus to be kind and tender-hearted to one another (Ephesians 4:32), but the sort of tender-hearted kindness which Paul envisaged has nothing to do with being soft, going along with anything in order to keep everyone happy. In fact, a few verses later (Ephesians 5:3–6) Paul names specific sins and goes on to warn his readers to 'have nothing to do with the fruitless deeds of darkness' (Ephesians 5:11), saying, 'Expose them.' It seems that we need to be prepared to make a stand, disagree, and even to upset people sometimes.

In reality, many attempts to spread happiness spring from the need to receive approval to make up for a lack of self-worth. Some folk need the approval of others so desperately that they are prepared to abandon their own likes and dislikes. This is often observed in teenagers. In order to feel more secure at a very vulnerable stage in growing up, many will adopt fashionable styles of clothing and tastes in music and change other aspects of their lives, hoping thereby to ensure the approval of their friends—or the 'in' people they would like to have as their friends. This behaviour is not unusual in adolescence, but some adults never leave it behind. 'What other people think' is their benchmark. They lack the confidence to develop their own tastes and views, in case someone disagrees with them or—horror of horrors—gets upset!

## Avoiding conflict at all costs

Some years ago I was present at a planning meeting at which it was agreed that Simon, a leader, would ask Naomi to take on a particular responsibility. Some days later I had a phone call from Naomi asking me to help her, which left me in no doubt that she had misunderstood the limits of her brief. I gently suggested that there might have been some misunderstanding, and encouraged Naomi to clarify things with Simon.

Naomi was pretty put out when I declined to take on the task she was trying to delegate to me—a task I was pretty sure was not hers to delegate—and even more put out because I dared to suggest that she might have misunderstood what was being asked of her. I confined myself to repeating my request that she check back with Simon. Later I checked that I was not the one who was mistaken. Simon confirmed that Naomi had misunderstood, adding: 'But don't tell her I said so!' I had had no intention of taking the matter further with Naomi, seeing that as his responsibility, but was concerned that he seemed to be heading for avoiding conflict rather than sorting out the confusion.

I heard nothing for a while, and then met Naomi at a teaching session, where she proceeded to announce to those around us during the coffee break that she supposed she had better forgive me for being so horrible to her by telling her she was mistaken! A mutual friend, Judith, became concerned because I seemed less than enthusiastic about being forgiven. As you may imagine, it all got rather complicated, as others unwittingly became involved in Simon's attempt to keep Naomi happy, and Naomi's less-than-happy response.

## *Allowing sin to remain unchallenged*

Bill, the manager of a small Christian conference centre, ran the ministry almost as an extension of his own person. When it was doing well, Bill basked in the glory, attributing the success to his management skills. When even trivial difficulties arose, every criticism or comment was a personal assault.

In reality, Bill was rather less capable than one might have imagined. The ministry only functioned effectively because of the good offices of numerous part-time employees, who went many 'extra miles' in order to keep the ministry on track. Andrew, a member of the board of trustees, became concerned about the unhealthy management style. He was also concerned because, from time to time, it appeared that Bill lied in an attempt to cover up his inadequacies. When Andrew eventually confronted Bill with his concerns, and recommended that he sought pastoral help, Bill became very angry and aggressive, telling further lies to boost his case.

The other trustees shared Andrew's concerns about Bill's style, but were reluctant to accept that Bill was lying. They felt that

Andrew should have been more concerned to 'keep the peace' in order not to damage the ministry. In any case, there was the problem of a high staff turnover to consider...

Regrettably, I have come across several similar examples of Christian ministries within which sin which was common knowledge was allowed to continue unchallenged by the leadership. Not surprisingly, the ministries have been undermined by this.

# Paul's letter to the Galatians

Few of us really enjoy conflict. However, we can see from the second chapter of Paul's letter to the Galatians that Peter's attempt to avoid a confrontation was divisive in the early church. Peter had been eating with Gentiles (something Jews were not permitted to do) but when visitors from Jerusalem arrived, Peter drew back and separated himself from them (Galatians 2:12). Paul had publicly confronted Peter (Galatians 2:11), insisting that, whatever some people in Jerusalem might be thinking, Jewish Christians must welcome uncircumcised Gentile Christians into full fellowship. The rest of the letter to the Galatians has this as a backdrop. One can sense a certain amount of frustration in Paul's final word on the subject in Galatians 6:15: 'Neither circumcision nor uncircumcision means anything; what counts is a new creation.'

If you can, please take a few minutes now to read the letter for yourself, as it contains teaching which touches on several of the issues discussed in this book—not just the matter of conflict among Christians.

## *Pleasing God rather than men*

Several years ago I reread Galatians whilst in the process of preparing some counselling teaching material on the subject of people-pleasing. The relevance of what Paul had written hit me very forcibly. There is a sort of black humour in the verse from Galatians quoted at the start of this chapter. Paul was no people-pleaser! He wrote to the Thessalonians in similar vein: 'We are not trying to please men but God, who tests our hearts' (1 Thessalonians 2:4) and 'We were not looking for praise from men, not from you or anyone else' (1 Thessalonians 2:6). To the Christians at Corinth he wrote: 'It matters very little to me what you think of me, even less where I rank in popular opinion. I don't even rank myself' (1 Corinthians 4:3, *The Message*).

Jews had been taught by God to keep themselves separate from other nations, but Jesus had made it clear that such divisions were no longer to exist among his followers. Peter seems to have gone along with this initially but then changed his mind. What made him so vulnerable to pressure (spoken or simply imagined) from others, such that he went so far as to distance himself from his Gentile brothers and sisters in Christ? In contrast, Paul seems to have been confident that he was on the right track, even in the face of disapproval from influential Jewish Christians. What made the difference? Was it their different calling from God (Paul to the Gentiles, Peter to the Jews)? Was Peter simply trying to protect his reputation among Jews in order not to hinder the gospel, or was there more to it?

I can imagine Paul putting the cat amongst the pigeons at many church ministry selection committees today! He saw God's call and commissioning as what counted; no other commissioning was necessary. It would appear (Galatians 1:16–17) that there might have been some expectation that, after his dramatic conversion, he would go up to Jerusalem to see the apostles for official validation. But he didn't. Three years later he went there, stayed with Peter and met up with James. He was happy to record (Galatians 2:9) that James, Peter and John eventually gave him (and Barnabas) the right hand of fellowship, having 'recognized the grace' given to him. But there was no sense of his needing their personal approval—rather the contrary!

## Freedom not slavery

I believe that an important thread through Paul's letter to the Galatians is that of freedom in Christ—freedom from slavery. Remember the origin of the word addict? (See page 18.) I don't think that Paul was setting out to be deliberately discourteous to those apostles of longer standing in the church. However, I do believe that he was intent upon nipping in the bud two very damaging trends: firstly, the tendency to seek a counterfeit form of righteousness in keeping regulations, and, secondly, focusing too much on human leaders (a theme also taken up in the first chapter of 1 Corinthians).

Paul was intent upon separating the newborn church from the tendency to rely on externals which had crept into Judaism over the centuries. As early as Deuteronomy 10:16 God wanted to emphasize 'circumcision of the heart' (that is, a heart-attitude corresponding to an outward physical sign) but this emphasis seems to have been overlooked. Christians were apparently heading down the same road, and Paul was seriously perturbed. Can't you hear the desperation in his voice as he dictates his letter? 'It is for freedom that Christ has set us free. Stand firm, then, and do not let yourselves be burdened again by a yoke of slavery. Mark my words! I, Paul, tell you that if you let yourselves be circumcised, Christ will be of no value to you at all' (Galatians 5:1–2).

# Doing the right thing

Having a particular church leader as an infallible reference point, or finding security in doing the right thing by keeping a certain set of regulations, is a 'yoke of slavery' which robs us of the freedom for which Christ set us free. If our eyes are on another person, watching out for signs of their approval, or are fixed on their prescribed list of dos and don'ts, they will not be on Christ.

In Galatians (Galatians 6:3–4) Paul advocates honest self-examination, but he wants us to avoid the league-table mentality which is only interested in whether we're doing better or worse than those around us. To the Colossians Paul writes of the 'mystery, which is Christ in you, the hope of glory' (Colossians 1:27). If we are continually looking at other people in order to know if we are doing better or worse than them, we shall be neglecting to attune our ear to our internal reference point, which is 'Christ in us', and neglecting to search the scriptures for guidance and wisdom.

## *Facing unpopularity*

Slavishly doing what others tell us is the right thing won't work when people hold differing opinions about the nature of 'the right thing'. In some matters the scriptures leave no room for manoeuvre; in others they are unfortunately inconclusive or even silent.

Take the matter of church music. Some Christians sincerely believe that the pipe organ is the only instrument fitting to accompany divine worship. Others find organ music deeply offensive because of its associations with what they judge to be sterile ritual.

As I see it, the wisdom of Solomon and the patience of Job would not be sufficient to keep people with these extreme views happy simultaneously in the same worship service! Yet most church leaders are faced with similar conflicts, often several at a time, and how they handle them will depend, amongst other things, on where their security lies.

Pastors have a difficult task. They have a responsibility for the well-being of individuals in their flock, and they know to some extent who is hurting and who is vulnerable. They feel a responsibility to lead forward the *whole* flock, while knowing that moving forward may cause them to lose contact with or in other ways hurt individuals. The loss may cause them deep personal pain, and may even cause them (or others) to doubt their calling. This pain is all the more intense if their security is external, and they use other people as their main point of reference. Is it possible that some church leaders work so hard because they are always trying to dull this very pain, striving for a level of approval which is impossible in such a ministry?

Church leader and author Jamie Buckingham writes:

> *It seems that ever since I became a Christian someone has been criticizing me. For the first dozen years of my Christian life I was criticized because I wasn't spiritual enough. In looking back on my life, I realize the criticism was justified. For the last dozen years... I have been criticized for being too spiritual, too radical, too enthusiastic, too charismatic, too honest. There are times when I just sit back and shake my head. Thank God I don't have to please everybody. Thank God I don't have to please anybody.*

Jamie Buckingham, *Coping with Criticism*

## *Doing whatever people appear to want*

What about the 'ordinary' men and women in a church fellowship? I never cease to be amazed at the pressure to which some folk willingly subject themselves in order to keep others happy.

I remember attending a house group leaders' meeting many years ago. I can't recall what we were talking about, but I remember saying that if a member of my group telephoned me for a chat just as one of my children had spilt Ribena on the carpet I would feel free to ask if I could phone back when I had cleared it up. This produced a wide-eyed shock reaction from another leader, who felt that one had a Christian duty to act sacrificially and receive phone calls however inconvenient the moment.

I know how I feel if I have been talking about non-urgent matters for a while to someone I consider a friend, and then discover that it has been extremely inconvenient. I feel hurt by their lack of honesty; they definitely have not kept me 'happy'!

On countless occasions men and women have confided in me that they would dearly love to extricate themselves from an undertaking which they accepted in order to please someone. They knew even at the time they accepted it that it wasn't right, or would be impossible for them to fulfil. Now they are living with the consequences. If only they had been honest enough, courageous enough, to use the 'N' word—that little word which begins with N and ends with O.

## Great expectations

From time to time I tell a good friend that I'm feeling called to found 'Recluse Ministries'. Can you visualize the scene? Based on a remote island (although having electricity and all other necessary requirements, of course) I would sit at my word-processor, writing, then take a break and wander out to enjoy the peace and tranquillity of the wide open spaces. Occasionally I would venture off the island to meet people by appointment, but I would always return within a day or two. 'Recluse Ministries' is my shorthand way of saying that I'm finding people's needs or expectations pressing in on me. (No doubt there are times in every family when one or other parent feels the same calling, and that's without the added pressures of work or church commitments!)

## 'I feel called to get away from it all'

It's important that I do acknowledge how I feel about the pressures. It prompts me to examine whether I might have been contributing to them by saying 'Yes' when I should really have been saying 'No', or whether I might have failed to build in the people-free spaces which I know I need to recharge my batteries. (Some find solitude draining and are energized by interacting with others, so their approach will be different.) Being honest about how I feel when pressures are mounting enables me to pay attention to my feelings, and to take any necessary action. It also helps me to distinguish them from the leading of the Holy Spirit, who as yet has *not* mentioned founding Recluse Ministries!

If we squash our feelings and refuse to acknowledge them (and so fail to take account of the fact that they *are* only feelings) it's all too easy to confuse them with God's voice. God does sometimes give us desires in our hearts which are at one with his purposes, and he does sometimes speak to us through our feelings—but *the same feeling can convey a variety of messages*, and we need to check out what the message really is. An inclination building up within us, the feeling that it's right to go—or not to go—in a particular direction, needs testing. A lack of fulfilment in my present task, and a heaviness in my spirit might lead me to believe that I was in the wrong job, but that conclusion would need checking. Otherwise, I might rush off to found Recluse Ministries, when all the Lord was leading me to do was to take some time off!

## If I let the real 'me' out
## I'm bound to upset someone

For several years I've been responsible for running what our church calls *The Bodybuilding Course*. Using the scriptures, it emphasizes that, just as the parts of our physical bodies are different by design, our individuality has potential for strengthening the body of Christ—provided that we're prepared to accept our own and others' differences, rather than seeing them as a threat to our belonging together. Can you truly celebrate differences in your fellowship? Or do you have to minimize them—even crush them—in order to maintain an appearance of unity? Diversity is not an automatic threat to unity. Neither is burying our individuality a recipe for harmony.

We've found it really liberating to learn that we don't all have to be the same, to get enthusiastic about the same things, to be good at the same things. It's a relief to find that others in the body of Christ actually revel in things I find draining or boring. I'm only too pleased to let them enjoy getting on with them! Other people value the fact that I enjoy writing, and will happily ask me to write a report or a book review, or to cover something for the church magazine, rather than sweating over it themselves. (Study 4 at the end of the book gives opportunity for further study and reflection on the place of diversity within the body of Christ.)

## *Whose plan do we follow?*

As I have already made clear, individuality need not be a threat to unity. I now want to go further and say that, as far as the body of Christ is concerned, uniformity leads to *disability* (1 Corinthians 12:17). We can see that transforming every part of a body into a foot would frustrate the purposes of the head. 1 Corinthians 12 makes the point, with a certain amount of humour, that as far as the body of Christ is concerned uniformity would be a dead loss! Yet some Christians behave as if the church were a factory dedicated to the production of lots of identical body-parts (Christians), with God as the quality control supervisor, rejecting any product with non-standard characteristics.

During a recent run of *The Bodybuilding Course* we were discussing the importance of encouraging everyone to be themselves—the people God created them to be—rather than clones. 'God doesn't want Stepford Christians,' said Anita. (The film *The Stepford Wives* is about women being replaced by robotic copies with a mechanical devotion to their husbands.) God created us with our individuality and I believe that he delights in it. Some churches may find our individuality hard to accommodate, but that's no reason for us to believe that God himself wishes us to be identically programmed clones who activate in standard ways at the flick of a master switch!

More than twenty years ago my husband and I attended a

church in which the women were allowed to do very little other than catering and helping with the children's work. I managed to avoid regular involvement with the latter— children's work is definitely not my area of expertise—but I felt under considerable pressure to participate in the annual children's holiday club, when it was a case of 'all hands on deck'. I was saved by the fact that I was working as a GP. When I told the organizers how much it would cost to pay for a locum to cover my surgeries while I helped with the club, they looked horrified and left me alone.

The other annual pressure was the obligation to rustle up mince pies at Christmas. My pastry is legendary—I mean that in the negative sense. In those days it wasn't possible to buy mince pies made by Mr Kipling or St Michael, so I worked hard to come up with something edible. For many years after we moved to another church, I carried with me the burden of failure—that I couldn't do what the church required of me.

## Whose expectations?

The pressure of other people's expectations can be very real, even a crushing weight, but it's important to be aware that sometimes the expectations we're hearing from others have their origins in our own hearts and minds. We may be projecting on to them the expectations we have of ourselves, and blaming them for pressure we have initiated.

Rachel was born in the 1930s, and her childhood was marred by bombing and other horrors of war, as well as sexual abuse. She was sent away to a convent when she was four years old, and attended thirteen different schools in eleven years. Having written to me about her many years of struggling with workaholism, Rachel has given me permission to tell her story.

God had featured in her life from an early age, but not as loving —just there and aware of her existence. Aged sixteen, Rachel made a confession of faith, and threw herself into church activity—never saying 'No' to anything which had God's name attached to it. In her teens she was teaching, preaching and leading the youth work. You name it, Rachel did it! She was persuaded to go to theological college and to be ordained. The loneliness and demands of the work soon began to tell on her body and mind, and spiritually she felt a hypocrite, whilst being seen as a 'success'. It was not acceptable to confess weakness or need if you were a leader! Rachel spent many lonely hours on her knees in the church, crying out to God in despair.

Rachel left the ministry, and began a series of jobs which involved caring for others. 'I always said that I had one thing to offer my employers which might make up for lack of expertise: I was conscientious!' But for Rachel this was a bondage, not a virtue. She would beaver away, far beyond expectations or job descriptions, and was always the last person to go home. Her energetic style was admired and welcomed, in the church as well as elsewhere. But every so-called success only made it worse. As Rachel never saw what she did as good enough, she continually feared failure and rejection. If she had managed to get something right, then everyone was surely going to expect her to do it again, and she might not be able to do so. 'I had terrifying nightmares. I moved to a new part of the country, and the leader of the church where I settled discerned my need to lay down all the roles behind which I'd been hiding—to "nestle, not wrestle", as one of my favourite saints, Corrie Ten Boom, said.'

Over the past ten years, Rachel has found much release and healing. Of this period she writes:

> It has been a most difficult and painful process, and I'm still caught off guard at times. In the end, my frenzied activity led to burn-out. The Lord chose to take away everything. He spoke to me tenderly and won my heart. He showed me that if I never did another thing he would still love me. He could forgive and heal me, and had a purpose for me. Even to this day I feel (rather like an alcoholic) that I'm only one step away from the workaholic treadmill. I still feel more comfortable with people if I'm fulfilling some need. I haven't yet learned how to relate securely without a role, but I'm asking the Lord to lead me on in this.

Yes, people did have great expectations of Rachel, but much of the pressure to do and to succeed came from within. As a child she'd learned that as soon as you attached yourself to an adult they were likely to send you somewhere else, so she tried hard to make them want to keep her with them. This, combined with the sexual

abuse forced on her from the age of six, left her with great difficulty in building relationships.

Sadly, the church failed to spot her immense neediness, and
compounded the problem for many years. When folk are as
willing to help as Rachel, it's tempting for hard-pressed church
leaders to allow them to get on with it, but it's vital that they resist the temptation, and lovingly confront what lies behind the
drivenness—for the sake of the individuals involved, but also
because allowing Christians to be driven beyond God's call does
not honour him. The good news is that it's never too late to step
off the treadmill and start receiving healing!

# How did Jesus handle it?

There's no doubt that people *did* have great expectations of Jesus.
How did he handle the pressures upon him? So many needing
healing. People with ideas about what he ought to be doing and
how he ought to be doing it!

## *'Time out' amidst the pressures*

Jesus and his followers walked a lot—there wasn't much option in
their day—and I don't believe that every step of the way would
have been in earnest conversation. Jesus' illustrations show that
he had a sense of humour—for example, the one about a man
with a plank in his eye remarking on the speck of sawdust in
someone else's (Matthew 7:3–4); he was making a serious point,
but the humour added poignancy. On other occasions I'm sure
that humorous exchanges between Jesus and the disciples will
have added to their relaxation. If you haven't noticed Jesus' sense
of humour, try rereading the gospels in an idiomatic version such
as *The Message*.

Jesus spent time staying with friends, and visiting their homes
for meals. Although he encouraged the disciples to stick with him,
Jesus also knew the value of solitude. In Luke 5:16 we read that
'Jesus often withdrew to lonely places and prayed'. When reading
Mark's account of the feeding of the five thousand it's easy to
overlook Jesus' concern that his disciples were being overwhelmed. 'Come with me by yourselves to a quiet place and get

some rest,' Jesus urged them (Mark 6:31). Later (Mark 6:45) he sent them on ahead while he dismissed the crowd, and then took time out to be alone with his Father (Mark 6:46).

## Following the Father's plan

Jesus knew that there would always be people clamouring for his attention—many of them in desperate need. But he did not allow this awareness to set his agenda. John's Gospel has a recurring emphasis: that Jesus did only what he saw the Father doing, and said only what the Father gave him to say. (John 5:19; 8:28; 12:49 and 14:24)

Jesus had free will, and used it to choose to follow the way the Father set before him, even though it led to the cross. In no sense was he driven there. Along the way, he acknowledged his feelings about what lay ahead. He didn't pretend it was going to be easy. He didn't go to the cross with an artificial smile on his face. Afterwards he showed his disciples the real wounds in his hands and his side.

If we practise listening to God—as we go about our daily activities, as well as in church—we won't become automatons. We'll still have to choose which path to follow—and we probably won't be short of alternative suggestions, especially when God is asking us to do something difficult or uncomfortable! If you find listening to God difficult, or the idea is new to you, you may find it helpful to read further about it. I can recommend Joyce Hugget's book *Listening to God*, in which she writes of her own, sometimes bumpy, journey of discovery.

## Jesus upsetting people

Jesus' insistence on following the Father's lead brought him into much conflict. Were you brought up to believe that upsetting people is inherently 'wrong'? Many have been taught that it is. Some would see this 'let's not upset anyone' approach to life as 'Christian'. However, even a quick flip through one of the gospels will reveal that Jesus Christ, from whom the adjective 'Christian' is derived, frequently upset people. Jesus chose to oppose the powerful leaders. He would have nothing to do with schemes which involved setting him up as a figurehead in the battle to oust the Romans. 'I do not accept praise from men,' he said (John 5:41). He chose to obey God.

Sometimes Jesus antagonized people because he was not prepared to tolerate the corrupt religion being peddled by the religious experts of his day. Jesus was aware that when he went to the synagogue (Mark 3:1) he was being watched by those who were keen to catch him out. Would he go against the official teaching and heal someone on the Sabbath? Mark records (3:5) that Jesus looked round in *anger* and was deeply distressed at their stubborn hearts. He had challenged them on their interpretation of the Law, and he went on to heal the man on the Sabbath, before their very eyes. 'He's got to go,' they said, and plotted how to get rid of him. Jesus had upset important people… he continued to upset important people. Jesus' confronting of ungodly leadership is dealt with in greater detail in chapter 6.

I have read several stories portraying how we might respond to Jesus if he were to appear today in our neighbourhood. For example, Gerard Hughes records an imaginary letter written by a desperate parish priest to his superiors. His life is being turned upside-down by a certain Mr E. Manuel (aged thirty-three) who has been applying for acceptance into religious orders and congregations. This politically naïve young man of dubious parentage associates with disreputable types, and holds open-air meetings at which liberal quantities of food are sometimes provided. A warrant is out for his arrest after he created a scene outside the Cathedral —something about overturning the bookstall table. The priest writes that Mr E. Manuel 'would have a devastating effect on any seminary or religious house imprudent enough to accept him' (Gerard Hughes, *God of Surprises*). I'm sure he's right.

So, is keeping people happy 'a Christian virtue'? It would seem not. But neither is upsetting everyone! The point is not that Jesus upset people so we should too, but that Jesus obeyed his Father— regardless of whether this pleased or enraged people—and we should too. Given that we sometimes make mistakes, and our understanding of God's will is at best imperfect, we would be well advised to check with the scriptures and probably some mature Christian friends if we are about to take an irrevocable leap into a cauldron of controversy. (Some major confrontations require an immediate and unprepared response, but many can be seen from some way off, and can be approached prayerfully, with an opportunity to hear others' wisdom on the matter.) Ultimately, we alone are responsible to God for our actions. People's opinions and strong reactions may be influential now, but they will count for very little in eternity.

# Focus point

**'Do I take "the real me" to church?'**

If not, why not?

**'Do I need to learn to use the N word more often?'** (The small word that begins with N and ends with O.)

**'How would I have responded?'**

Some of the religious leaders *did* choose to follow Christ. Others would have liked to have done so, but feared the disapproval of important people (John 12:42–43). It's easy to look back scornfully and be sure that we'd have welcomed Jesus and stood by him through thick and thin, whatever anyone said or did to us. Would we really? Let's be open to the Lord showing us if we are compromising in order to keep people happy (or for any other reason), and ask him to give us the grace and strength to seek his approval alone.

# 5

# What about worship?

### Psalm 16:11

*You will fill me with joy in your presence...*

Worshipping the Lord, in song and in other ways, is a mood-altering activity. I'm glad it is! J.B. Phillips expresses the meaning of Ephesians 5:18–19 as follows: 'Don't get your stimulus from wine (for there is always the danger of excessive drinking), but let the Spirit stimulate your souls. Express your joy in singing among yourselves psalms and hymns and spiritual songs, making music in your hearts for the ears of the Lord!'

This chapter is not intended as a criticism of any particular style of worship, but as a reminder that aspects of the *process* of worship have the potential for being misused by fallen and needy human beings. *Anything* that is mood-altering, or which is used as a distraction from painful realities, has the potential for addictive misuse. The idea that worship could be so misused is particularly disturbing because true worship is meant to be a way of reverencing the source of all that is good.

## The feel-good factor

In liturgical traditions regular worshippers may 'feel better' for hearing the well-known words, listening again to the telling out of timeless truths, and going through the changes of posture according to a well-rehearsed pattern. They will experience the familiar sounds, the smell of flowers (maybe of incense) and perhaps even the reassuring mustiness of a building that has stood for centuries as a witness to the faith.

In other fellowships the words are never the same two weeks running and worshippers never know quite what is coming next, but the air of expectancy is the same each week. The band plays a variety of music—some lively, some reflective—and everyone is encouraged to respond by clapping, dancing, kneeling or prostrating themselves, releasing tears or laughter, or speaking out a word from God to the other worshippers.

## Perfect worship?

As a teenager I sang in the church choir, and I remember a special occasion on which we were invited to lead a service in Rochester Cathedral. During the administration of communion we sang two anthems. We were very nervous, but, as we sang, something happened. It was if God was taking our offering of praise and worship and transforming it into something exquisitely beautiful—far beyond anything we'd ever achieved in practice sessions. More than being musically in tune, it felt spiritually 'in tune' too. I remember almost nothing about the rest of the day, but the sense of God inspiring our worship stays with me.

Yes, it was awesome. Yes, it did feel good, but 'good' in the sense of pure and unalloyed, rather than merely pleasant. I've experienced it on numerous occasions since, in a variety of places—none of them cathedrals! Perhaps the only common thread I *can* see is that of unexpectedness. On each occasion it was as if God sovereignly intervened. It wasn't the immense talent of the person leading the service, or of others who were participating. It was like the transforming of the loaves and fishes into a feast for a multitude—something miraculously greater than the sum of the parts.

By contrast, human efforts at perfection in worship can be incredibly depressing. Where traditional worshippers are earnestly seeking to put on the 'perfect' act of worship, faultlessly recreating something which has been handed down through the centuries, it can be disappointingly sterile if the worshippers are paying more attention to the crossed t's and dotted i's of the liturgy than to the one whom they're supposed to be worshipping. Some seem to find an unhealthy security in the repetition, becoming unduly anxious if any part is omitted. They need to know what's coming next, and that it'll be the same as last week and last year. The worship feels dangerously out of control if it isn't.

No less depressing are the efforts of an enthusiastic team using a modern style if they're merely cranking the handle of the all-singing all-dancing worship machine, trying to create the right buzz. Aiming to reproduce last week's holy glow or roof-raising euphoria—and becoming anxious if nothing seems to be happening—may be culturally a world away from the sterility described above, but spiritually it probably has much in common.

Sloppy, ill-prepared leading of worship and a *laissez-faire* attitude to, for example, the standard of music played in services ought to be discouraged. Yet we need to recognize that the temptation to strive for 'perfect worship' can be very great. Worship offered in the spirit of perfectionism is the antithesis of true worship; it can come close to worshipping the worship. So-called worship, in which our needs for significance or control are calling the tune, or which is driven by perfectionism, is putting self on the throne, not God.

God-centred worship can be not just mood-altering but profoundly life-changing; telling out God's worth can change our whole perspective, but there's a very real sense in which the outcome of any time of worship cannot be guaranteed. It's up to us to do all that we know needs doing in terms of repenting, and come before God with clean hearts and willing spirits, but the rest is up to him. God's participation in our worship cannot be programmed or timetabled, and we believe otherwise at our peril.

## *Healthy expectancy, healthy scepticism*

Over the past thirty years there has been a revolution in worship in the Church of England and in many other denominations, and much of it has been for the better. The gradual change to using modern language services and Bible translations has given a greater understanding of what is being said. There is more participating and less spectating. Greater expectancy can reduce the 'same again' feel of worship services, even where much of the familiar pattern has been retained. In addition, this has allowed many people to experience physical and emotional healing, especially in churches where prayer ministry is on offer for those who would like to receive it.

However, an element of healthy scepticism is required: not all that happens, even in the most 'Spirit-filled' churches, is 'of the Spirit'. In addition to being spiritual, we are emotional *and* cerebral *and* physical beings, and not totally redeemed in our behaviour, thoughts and feelings. We need to be honest and ask ourselves (individually and corporately) if we are really worshipping in spirit and in truth (John 4:23). Or are we allowing the flesh, in one way or another, to call the tune? We're all fallible human beings, and it's easy enough for our fallenness to shape our worship.

# Checking out the focus

God wants us to worship him with the whole of our being. That includes our emotions. We need to go on saying 'Yes!' to our emotions being involved in worship, but we also need to be on our guard against allowing emotions and sensory experiences to hijack the focus. (In some traditions, the cerebral has been allowed to hijack the focus for too many years, and this is just as unhealthy!)

The danger comes when the *experience* of meeting with God, the sensations and emotions associated with his presence, are central in focus, taking the place of God himself. It is only too easy to end up idolizing the experience rather than worshipping the creator.

## *Creating an atmosphere*

There is much to be said for encouraging a congregation to unite in a co-ordinated act, all worshipping in a particular way at a particular time. However, there are occasions on which I have wondered if perhaps a worship leader was being unduly manipulative, dictating the congregation's physical posture (standing reaching out to God, kneeling in adoration), telling everyone what to say to God, and what God is saying back, and so on. They might have been horrified if someone had pointed out to them that instructions and prescribed prayers of this type were common in the old service books with which they have so cheerfully dispensed!

Using the same sort of instructions, a worship leader may contrive an atmosphere which brings about the release of emotions—for example, tearful sadness or exuberant joy. He will be particularly vulnerable in this regard if he allows his own emotions to surface only when he is worshipping. And I write *his* and *he* because in my experience this happens more often with men than with women. Encouraging people to find emotional release is not automatically wrong, but placing an exaggerated emphasis on the expression of emotions may distract people from what they're meant to be doing—worshipping!—and from what God is seeking to do by his Spirit. Putting the focus on emotions can prompt carbon-copy expectations, and contrived 'me too' responses. 'Thou shalt not covet' thy neighbour's overwhelming emotional experience, and mimic it for fear of feeling left out. We all need to be reminded to seek God rather than experiences.

We need to teach that it's OK to release emotions in worship, but to go on to teach the difference between the spiritual and the emotional. All Christians need to learn to recognize God's presence, and to differentiate between what is of God and what just feels nice. It's not difficult to manipulate people. The power of suggestion can be used to mimic experiences of the presence of God. This is dangerous. It opens the way to all sorts of abuse, and is directly contrary to God's purposes. It is sensation-seeking, not worshipping God. I believe that it is abhorrent to God, and damaging to his church, because, although it has the trappings of worship, it is a counterfeit.

## A dangerous confusion

If someone's emotions are normally kept locked away, but are allowed to surface during worship, they may find this pleasant; if the emotions are painful ones, they may welcome the resulting release which makes way for more pleasant emotions. If they fail to understand the difference between the spiritual and the emotional, they may confuse experiencing pleasant emotions with experiencing the presence of God. This will have a variety of consequences, one of which is that they may end up believing that God is absent unless they are experiencing pleasant emotions. They can become fearful and feel abandoned when their emotions dip from a peak.

If this happens, they may crave re-immersion in whatever experiences they have found most likely to recreate the feelings.

The opposite can also be believed: that pleasant emotions are a sign of God's presence and his blessing upon us wherever we are and whatever we are doing. Thinking in that way, a married doctor who preached in his home church was sure that his affair with a clerical assistant (who was a Christian) was ordained by God because it felt so good. He went on to abandon the Bible, assuring everyone that he no longer needed it because he was hearing God directly.

Pleasant feelings, such as joy and exhilaration, can be experienced when the Holy Spirit is at work during our worship, but we must beware of abusing worship by focusing on and pursuing the feelings. If religious activity is used compulsively in an effort to recreate a high, the effect is to practise the presence of the addiction. At best, this could be seen as idolizing religious experience; at worst, enthroning sin and sickness and calling them by God's name.

## Emotions to order

'Look around the church and smile at one another. We're full of the joy of the Lord, aren't we?' From time to time I have been in a Christian meeting or church service when something of this sort has been said by a leader. Sometimes it has been prefaced by a comment about how miserable everyone is looking, or about how the said responses or the singing lack the expected gusto. Seeing smiling faces may reassure the leader that all is well, and may even give a lift to some flagging spirits, but I am as uneasy about lying to one another with our facial muscles as I am about lying with our words.

Adrian Plass writes of a worship leader who, carried away with his own enthusiasm, instructed the congregation to give 'a spontaneous round of applause' after the next chorus. Adrian Plass goes on: 'That kind of thoughtless comment arises, more often than not, from a fear that things are not "buzzing" spiritually in the way one might expect if God was really present in the service or meeting. Insecure leaders will occasionally project their fears onto those they are leading' (Adrian Plass, *View From a Bouncy Castle*).

He goes on to relate a story about a church elder he used to know who had a habit of interrupting services, usually mid-song, with the diagnosis that there was 'a "spirit of heaviness" in the room that was preventing people from worshipping freely'. Of course, having made that declaration, he was then in need of someone doing something in response (bursting into tears, or crying out in repentance). Adrian Plass observes: 'I'm certainly not suggesting that the Holy Spirit doesn't or can't work in situations like that, but inciting others to produce spiritual-type behaviour as a means of reassuring ourselves is surely not terribly constructive.'

## *Leading—or controlling?*

Many leaders rightly encourage awareness of the presence of God when worshipping. However, it's vital that in so doing they're generating an expectancy which is focused on God—not stimulating a Pavlovian-type response focused on cues given out by the worship leader. There's an important difference between *leading* and *controlling* worship. If worship is controlled rather than led, there's real danger that the congregation will learn to perform to order, rather than to respond to what God is doing. It's good to check out the focus of worship: to what extent is the worship leader central? It's possible, indeed desirable, to lead worship without everyone's attention being focused on us!

Having a worship *team* rather than a single individual taking responsibility for worship is of great benefit—provided that the team is one within which members are allowed to play their full part. If it is dominated by one or two strong personalities who are determined to make certain things happen, a team can drive a fellowship even more relentlessly in an unhealthy direction.

It's easy to be always looking forward, anticipating the requirements for the next service or event. It can be valuable to take a few moments to review before pressing on. How did last Sunday's service go? Did we get it right—spiritually, not just structurally, liturgically, or musically? What went particularly well? Did anyone feel uneasy about anything? Has there been any feedback from the wider leadership or the congregation? When we pray together, what particularly do we need to give thanks for? Do we need to say sorry to God (or to one another) for anything?

Music team leaders and members need to have spiritual insight as well as musical gifts, and they need to be willing to take a servant role under the authority of the overall church leadership. I used to hear of clergy struggling to work with a choir and organist who behaved as if they were running the church; now I'm starting to hear of similar problems involving music teams!

# Worshipping in truth as well as in spirit

It seems that God's people have always been tempted to try to isolate their worship from the reality of their lives and the world around them. Jesus was quoting Isaiah 29:13 when he said (Matthew 15:8; Mark 7:6): 'These people honour me with their lips, but their hearts are far from me.'

Thinkers from a variety of traditions and across the centuries have sought to convince us that true spirituality (and therefore true worship) can only inhabit a plane which is divorced from everything physical. For example, first-century Christians came under the influence of Greek thinkers who reasoned that, as everything physical is evil, Jesus Christ could not possibly have had a real physical body. Many people are unaware of the extent to which our own culture has absorbed this sort of thinking, which is a far cry from the integrated spirituality which Jesus taught and demonstrated.

Worshippers have real bodies, which play their part in worship —sitting, standing, kneeling, vocalizing, receiving the bread and wine, and so on. Last year I damaged my knee in a fall, and was temporarily unable to do some of these things. It didn't stop me worshipping but I felt restricted, and on the first Sunday after the accident the pain was quite distracting. If I had been taking my lead from the Greeks, I might have concluded that the only answer was to worship God on a higher spiritual plane, allowing myself to be transported to a realm in which knees—bruised and swollen or otherwise—had no place. Yes, at times we may be so aware of God's presence that all physical distractions pale into insignificance, but this is different from maintaining that the physical has no place in worship.

In the same way, worshippers have real thoughts and feelings which cannot automatically be left behind when coming to worship—nor is it intended that they should be! There is an important sense in which we need to worship God from where we are, rather than from where we'd like to be. For example, if we're having a rough time with family illness and job uncertainties, we need to set our hearts to worship him while surrounded by the difficulties. We can't pretend the difficulties don't exist—they do! And we and God know they do! But we can choose to worship God for who he is, which is the same in our bad times as in our good times, and to thank him for his faithfulness. Worship can raise our spirits in all sorts of ways—the reading of scripture, praise and thanksgiving, singing, and so on. It can give us a glimpse of heavenly realities far beyond our imagination, and lift us up so that we see our lives from a new standpoint. But the person offering the worship to God has to be the real me, the person who is struggling—I can't send some fantasy super-spiritual alter-ego who has no experience of any problems to worship on my behalf!

Speaking to the Samaritan woman at the well, Jesus said:

> 'It's who you are and the way you live that count before God. Your worship must engage your spirit in the pursuit of truth. That's the kind of people the Father is out looking for: those who are simply and honestly themselves *before him in their worship. God is sheer being itself—Spirit.* Those who worship him must do it out of their very being, their spirits, their true selves, in adoration.'

(John 4:23–24, *The Message*)

## *Feel what you feel*

Some people speak as if troublesome emotions, such as fear or anger, were automatically sinful, and as such shouldn't be felt by Christians, let alone brought to church! I've heard people preach that fear and anger are sin—but is pretending we're not afraid or angry so much more spiritual?

On the contrary, if someone acknowledges their fears to God, this action can make them more open to receiving the gifts of faith and hope, which will enable them to confront painful realities. In expressing their fears to God, they will be turning their hearts and minds to him. This will help them to take their eyes off their fears. Sometimes anger is justified and is a prompting to righteous action; more often it isn't. Bringing it before God will help to sort out which it is. The fears and anger aren't buried, but they are no longer central—God is.

Unacknowledged strong emotions can block hearing God, or lead us to believe that we're hearing him when we're hearing ourselves. The acknowledgment of fear or anger can clear the channels so that we can more easily hear what God *is* saying—which may be that we've taken a wrong route, or allowed sin to creep into our lives. Feelings can be messengers that say 'something's wrong here'. If they cause us to pause long enough to hear what God has been trying to get through to us, they will have done us a valuable service.

Acknowledging troublesome feelings also opens the way for God to act. (Sometimes that *will* allow us to return home feeling much better.) Fake super-spirituality that edits out all these troublesome emotions misses out on the benefits, and is creating a dangerous gap between our inner selves and the way we appear to be.

## *The pain of loss*

Grief is another emotion on some people's hit list; they want to do away with it because they see grief when a loved one dies as evidence of lack of faith. Or perhaps it's just too embarrassing or uncomfortable to have around—we have an urge to tidy it up and make it better. No, we don't grieve in the same way as those who have no hope (1 Thessalonians 4:13), but grief and loss on parting come with love. A reunion to come one day doesn't remove the pain of separation now. Far from being 'a wonderful Christian witness', the total absence of grief when a loved one dies is evidence of something wrong somewhere.

We need to be able to acknowledge and to share one another's grief, publicly in worship services (with due sensitivity) as well as privately. We need, corporately as well as individually, to support those left behind as they make faltering steps into a life which in a very real sense will never be the same again. It *won't* be the same—but that doesn't mean life won't go on: it will be different, in some respects painfully so, but it *will* go on. Pretending that everything's OK and that nothing has changed is evidence of denial, not of faith.

## Rejoicing with those who rejoice

'Feeling what you feel' also needs to apply to joyous emotions. Some fear that they'll be seen as bragging, and are reluctant to share their high points. They may also be aware that others are struggling, and not want to appear to be unsympathetic to their problems.

We're told to 'rejoice with those who rejoice' in the same sentence as we're told to 'mourn with those who mourn' (Romans 12:15). Of course we'll want to be sensitive, but in a strange way it's possible for very mixed emotions to co-exist. A time of prayer in which we intercede for those who are recently bereaved can also include thanks to God for blessings received.

## Come as you are

The church I attend operates a 'come as you are' policy. By that I mean that members are urged to come when they're feeling sad as well as when they're full of the joys of life, to bring their doubts as well as their fears. People are as welcome when they're having a bad day as when they're having a good day—in fact, it's even more important that they come on a bad day! Not everyone finds this easy to cope with. We all have days when we'd rather crawl into a hole, and sometimes we do just that and give church a miss.

Declaring God's faithfulness and reminding myself of his mercy and his love usually lifts my spirits, but occasionally I go to church feeling low, and come home feeling worse rather than better. 'Church' isn't a mood-altering drug with a guaranteed happy-making effect—but at least I know I've been with God's people, and, if I've managed to tell them I'm not feeling so good, I know they'll be praying.

However, some people are just plain difficult! Regardless of all the effort folk put into making them feel welcome and at home, they go on being prickly. They continue to feel unloved or unwanted, because the scars from painful past experiences make it hard for them to feel loved and accepted in the present—however friendly and caring people are. They may react by staying away from church, or by coming but always complaining about what they are seeing as a lack of welcome, or the leader's pastoral inadequacies—a projection of their feelings from the past rather than a reflection of genuine deficiencies.

We need to go on welcoming difficult individuals with genuine love and concern—however prickly they may be. A 'come as you are' policy needs to apply to them too. By accepting them—although not taking on their distorted perceptions—by praying for them, and showing Christ's love in action, we may help them to feel secure enough to let go of the past and find healing for their wounds.

# Personality and worship

Have you heard other people enthusing about an event that left you feeling bored, or found them strangely unmoved by something that really had you on the edge of your seat? What you or I relish may not be everyone's cup of tea, and even if we're both enjoying the same thing our ways of showing it may be completely different.

After many years of searching, Allan became a Christian on a trip to Israel. He returned to church with a big grin and a T-shirt saying 'I was baptized in the River Jordan'! There was much public rejoicing, and not a few tears of joy. That was Allan's style! Others who have become Christians have been no less joyful, but have preferred to share the news more quietly and individually—and haven't bought a colourful T-shirt to advertise their newfound faith.

Our different personalities will have an impact on our worship too. There is no single right and proper way to worship, and many of the disagreements in churches about worship would be less heated if there were greater understanding of personality—and greater generosity of spirit on the part of all concerned!

## *Predictability versus spontaneity?*

For some, part of the attractiveness of liturgical worship lies in its predictability. If our personality is such that we like routine, order-liness, knowing where we're going, and getting there with the minimum of fuss, this will be reflected in the type of worship which appeals to us. Other people's personalities are such that they find *all* routine stifling. Their attention will wander if any-thing's too predictable. They'll be attracted to variety and innova-tion in worship (and other activities) and will revel in all things new. They may even go so far as to see those who stress the need for worship to be conducted in an orderly fashion as 'quenching the Holy Spirit'.

It is regrettable that so often the answer to differing preferences is division. As far as worship is concerned, and in many other as-pects of life too, we really need one another! Every church needs members who will remind God's people that he is not pre-dictable—who will be alert for a sign that this week's best-laid plans are intended to go astray. (For example, it might become apparent while the preacher is preaching that a different song or hymn to follow would better sum up and expand on the message which God seems to be emphasizing at that particular time.) But every church also needs those who are aware of God's immutabil-ity, and who know that his purposes are not at the mercy of whim or fashion. We need leadership teams who will prayerfully plan themes and teaching programmes, and choose hymns and songs in time for the choir or music group practice. But within those teams we need individuals who will be alert to the possibility of a last-minute change of plan, and who won't be fazed by it.

Just as a heart-attitude of clinging blindly to set forms or pre-arranged plans can be a form of idolatry, so can the pursuit of all things new. Just because something's old/new, it doesn't mean it's better, or more holy. Just because something's pre-arranged/spon-taneous, it doesn't mean it's less likely to be used by the Lord.

## *Loud cymbals versus lute and harp?*

I find noise very tiring. Church services which attract large crowds can be very noisy, and I usually prefer the quieter ones. This is not a criticism of the services—merely a recognition that there are limits to what I can cope with in terms of noise.

I also prefer time for reflection. When there is a time of silence after a reading or the sermon to allow for reflection, I welcome it—knowing that others who are of a more activist disposition will be sitting there appreciating it rather less! As with so many other things, silence can be used out of habit, or even manipulatively, but, rightly used, it can be a powerful element of worship.

If we're of a certain temperament, it's easy to assume that God is always in the loud and the dramatic. When I read the account of Elijah's encounter with God, I enjoy noticing that on this occasion God seems to have chosen to appear in 'a gentle whisper' (AV: 'still small voice') rather than in the eardrum-thudding stuff that preceded his making himself known (1 Kings 19:11–13). If we're inclined to believe that drama and volume must equal spiritual potency, we need to develop our 'spiritual ears' to differentiate that which is of God from that which is just mighty impressive and gets the adrenaline going. Conversely, if we're comfortable with silence and have a marked preference for gentle whispers, we need to remember that peace and quiet are not synonymous with reverence; that is an attitude of the heart of the worshipper, and cannot be determined by the decibel level. God himself does sometimes encourage his people to 'make a joyful noise'!

# Worshipping together

A commitment to worshipping *together* with members of the body of Christ with different preferences is an important safeguard against the misuse of mood-altering worship. Each of us sees some facets of God's truth and purpose more clearly than others—we all have our blind spots—so it's easier to see the whole if we stick together.

In practice, worshipping together with people with different preferences often causes real difficulties, but many of them are far from insuperable. If Christians from different denominations are assembled together in one place, and each individual heart and mind is focused on the Lord, they can worship together. Sadly, too many hearts are more attuned to singing 'My Way' with Frank

Sinatra! Where difficulties are primarily a result of sinfulness—pride, self-seeking and so on—repentance is necessary.

## Together in diversity

The church I attend has three morning congregations, each with a different style of worship. The members of the leadership attend all three congregations (although not all on the same day) and usually the same sermon is preached by the same preacher at two of them. There is a degree of movement of individuals between the congregations, and this is to some extent encouraged. Recently, when an influx of visitors was expected to cause a crush at a special morning service held in the main church building, members were encouraged to consider attending one of the other congregations that week. Several house groups include individuals from more than one congregation, and pastoral care is organized through house groups and geographical groupings which deliberately take no account of the congregation with which people meet on Sundays.

There is one evening service in the main church building, which is attended by a relatively small number of folk from each of the three congregations. The past year has seen a wide variety of styles of worship at this service. We sing some of the old hymns alongside the newer songs. Liturgy (old and new) takes its place, but not to the exclusion of other ways of planning a service.

Yes, there are difficulties. No, not everyone is happy! I very much hope that attendance at the evening service will grow (although if everyone comes there won't be room). I hope we'll all learn to worship in a variety of ways, and come to recognize the difference between what is 'not of the Lord' and what is merely 'not my style'. I pray that we'll become more conscious of worshipping the Lord and less conscious of what style we're using at any given moment.

## Together—somewhere else?

Flitting from one church to another without making any commitment is to be discouraged, but it can be good to choose to worship in different surroundings from time to time. Try seeking God in surprising places! Do you find it possible to be aware of his presence without the familiar surroundings and patterns of worship? Visiting friends, or being away on a holiday or a retreat, provide obvious opportunities, but you could prayerfully consider seeking God in an unfamiliar place of worship locally—perhaps a church which uses a different style of worship or liturgy from your own. What emotions are provoked by this prospect? Anxiety? Fear? Horror? Perhaps relief. What thoughts come to mind?

Can you cope with the idea of meeting with God somewhere else, or have you come to believe (or been taught) that this is inconceivable? It may not be the right time for you to choose to experiment with meeting with God elsewhere. It may not be the right step for you at this stage of your faith, or for other reasons, but prayerfully thinking through the possibility—and recognizing the feelings this provokes—could prove very revealing.

There may be practical reasons why you're not free to vary your normal pattern of church attendance, but might you be able to vary your pattern of meeting with God on your own? Consider doing things in a different order, or in a different part of the house—or outside. If there's a park or a field nearby, you could make use of it occasionally, but it doesn't always have to be somewhere peaceful—meeting with God while walking the length of the high street might bring a new dimension to your worshipping and praying. Again, this might not be the right moment for you to experiment—especially if you've only recently begun to meet with God on your own. But if you've followed the same pattern of 'quiet time' for many years, today might be the day to set aside the security of the familiar and try a fresh approach. If you use Bible reading notes, a change of title can be helpful. If you always begin with the Bible and notes, try beginning with a time of silence. If the absence of the usual structure leaves you feeling anxious, tell God how you feel. If you're tempted to reach for your Bible and open it and start reading anywhere—anything to break the silence—tell God that too. And listen for what he has to say. He might be trying to tell you where to start...

## Together at last

In Psalm 86 (Psalm 86:9–10) David looks forward to the time when every tribe and tongue will be worshipping together. 'All the nations you have made will come and worship before you, O

Lord; they will bring glory to your name. For you are great and do marvellous deeds; you alone are God.' Not only will our church-manship squabbles be sidelined when this great day arrives, but all the international divisions will count as nothing too, because everyone is focusing on God and telling out his worth. Won't that be something!

David goes on (Psalm 86:11–12) to ask the Lord to teach him his way, and to give him an undivided heart. Let's echo that prayer, and allow weekly, daily, moment-by-moment worship to flow from lives which allow no artificial division between worship and life. As we worship from where we are, rather than from where we'd like to be, let's thank God for each new day and for his lov-ing mercy shown to sinners.

Worship is a mood-altering activity. It's meant to be! But it's so much more than that. As we continue to confront the issues raised in this chapter (which are further considered in Study 5 at the end of the book) and to explore options for change, let's not lose sight of whom we're worshipping and why.

# Focus point

J B Phillips' version of Ephesians 5:18 says 'let the Spirit stimulate your souls'.

**'Do I allow the Spirit to stimulate my soul?'**

**'Checking out the focus of my/our worship, what do I see?'**

If you're aware that the Lord has been speaking to you about something that's wrong, don't come under accusation—confess it to the Lord. Seek his cleansing, and help to put it right.

**'Have I been happy to allow others to worship in different ways?'**

Have you found other people's ways of worshipping threatening? Alternatively, have you felt obliged to worship in someone else's way, and so found it difficult to enter fully into worship? Bring the thoughts and emotions stimulated by these questions before God in prayer, and ask him to show you how he sees things.

# Authority and leadership

## Matthew 23:2—4

*'The teachers of the law and the Pharisees... tie up heavy loads and put them on men's shoulders, but they themselves are not willing to lift a finger to move them.'*

*We have used the Bible as if it was a constable's handbook—an opium-dose for keeping beasts of burden patient while they are being overloaded.*

Charles Kingsley (1819–74),
*Letters to the Chartists* No. 2

In most churches there are many different leadership roles: in addition to the minister or leadership team, there are those who shoulder responsibility for the youth work, the drama group, the flower arrangers' rota, and so on. It's also worth remembering that many people give a lead in the church and elsewhere without being officially called leaders. Those of us who are parents seek to exercise authority in the home, so thoughts about authority and leadership can apply to us too.

## Driven leadership

Churches are full of imperfect human beings and are led by imperfect leaders. All leaders make mistakes, some of which amount to misuse of their position. But some individuals are particularly prone to abusing their authority because of the disabling effects of their emotional pain. Their role is important to them because it provides the sense of identity they lack; they are desperate for the feelings of worth which come from a position of honour; they crave the buzz associated with having control over others. It is inevitable that the realities of their inner struggles will influence their leadership, however much they may try to keep them hidden.

It is sad that a leadership team with high aspirations can be effectively hamstrung by the unhealed wounds of one or two individuals. The team may speak of being led according to God's will and purpose, but if *in practice* the guiding rule is 'Don't rock the boat by disagreeing' or 'Don't upset the pastor' the Holy Spirit will not have free reign.

## Needing to succeed

Anyone who is desperate for other people's approval will make those around aware of this need—either consciously or subconsciously. Their body-language as well as their words will reflect their need for positive feedback and their distaste for anything remotely critical, however constructively framed. Maybe you've noticed that someone you know always stiffens at the first whiff of anything negative, furrowing their brow and giving out the sort of signals designed to discourage further unwelcome comment.

If someone is experiencing much pain from unhealed wounds, their sense of identity or self-worth can be located outside themselves, perhaps in a particular service or ministry—which therefore has to be a success, whatever it takes, in order to quieten inner voices of self-doubt. Their whole ministry—however genuinely selfless in its declared aims—can end up being driven by their own need to feel valued, significant, good about themselves. Some have reached positions of high responsibility largely as a by-product of their drivenness, flogging themselves to death in order to prove they're not the failures they secretly believe themselves to be. Strange as it may seem, having achieved an honoured position they feel no better about themselves; although they've succeeded in moving up the ladder they haven't changed on the inside—they feel they've no right to be there. The fear of being found out or letting people down can be very strong under these circumstances.

Yes—we all need encouragement from time to time, especially

if we're in a difficult role, such as church leadership. Positive feedback is always welcome, but it is best received in the context of a relationship within which it would be acceptable to be critical. Positive feedback is less valuable if that's the only sort of feedback allowed.

## Needing to control

Leaders can drive those they are leading harder and harder, looking not just for a good team effort but for a perfect result. Everyone starts to feel uneasy: their commitment is being extracted from them, rather than freely offered. They start to feel trapped, but they've received a lot of subtle messages about not letting the side down, so they soldier on.

They probably don't feel abused. They may indeed feel a bit ashamed of their own lack of enthusiasm. They probably feel weary. They may feel distant from God. But they don't bring any of these troublesome feelings to the surface, let alone speak them out. The watchword in such situations is *control*: don't think, don't feel—except what you're told you think and feel. And when the leader says that God is saying 'Do this' or 'Do that', do it straight away without questioning, because we all know that God can't abide disobedience.

Psalm 111 tells us: 'The fear of the Lord is the beginning of wisdom' (Psalm 111:10), but the fear of the Lord's *representatives* can have a less beneficial effect, especially if they are insecure and controlling. From a distance control can look like strong leadership, but closer examination—and perhaps also the passage of time—will reveal the difference. If those who are following are being stunted in their personal and spiritual growth, losing touch with who they are and where they're going, and are increasingly relying on their leader to tell them what to do, this is control. If God only speaks through certain people, is there not also a sense in which God is being controlled?

As Eugene Peterson writes in his introduction to Galatians in *The Message*:

> When men and women get their hands on religion, one of
> the first things they often do is turn it into an instrument for

*controlling others, either putting or keeping them 'in their place'.*
*The history of such religious manipulation and coercion is long*
*and tedious. It is little wonder that people who have only known*
*religion on such terms experience release or escape from it as free-*
*dom. The problem is that the freedom turns out to be short-lived.*

# Abusive systems

In past centuries, people were tortured to force them to embrace
the faith or cause of those who were in power. Where the alternative was a slow and painful death, changing allegiance became
understandably attractive. Abusive systems today may appear to
lack the life-and-death power wielded in past centuries, but in
practice they can be just as dangerous to those who have become
enmeshed in them. We might expect that in a free country such
abusive systems would fade away through lack of support, as
people vote with their feet. Sadly, those without a sense of their
personal identity can find them magnetically attractive. There is
always a queue of volunteers willing to tolerate a wide variety of
abuses in exchange for the security of knowing they belong somewhere and are somebody. Being an abused somebody who belongs somewhere feels preferable to being a nobody who belongs
nowhere.

## What are abusive systems?

Families, places of work, churches, groups and organizations of
any sort can function as abusive systems. Their key feature is that
individuals do not feel free to think their own thoughts, to feel
their own feelings, or to know what's good for them. There is no
true dialogue, and the flow of ideas is in one direction only. The
climate is such that few risk putting their head above the parapet;
they sense that it is not safe to do so.

Individuals who *do* ask questions, offer additional information
from 'outside', try to see things from a different point of view, or
who suggest that things might be done differently, are seen as
dangerously subversive. Anyone who challenges the behaviour or
management style of the leaders (be they parents, managers, or

church leaders) suddenly becomes the problem. Attempts will be made to bring them back into line, by manipulation, withdrawal of privileges or threats of disapproval. If this fails they will eventually be forced out or thrown out.

### Out of the frying-pan into the fire

Vulnerable people often go from one abusive system to another. For example, a teenage girl may break out of a family in which she has felt pressurized to conform and unable to establish her own identity, only to end up in the grip of a cult. Her new 'family' claims to offer the ultimate security of knowing the true road to enlightenment, and is led by a guru whose wisdom is beyond question. Being so unlike her home environment it will seem an attractive alternative, but it will be just as abusive (especially if the road to enlightenment includes sex with the leader), and will further stunt her growth towards full personhood.

Teenage girls on the run from their families can end up in other abusive sexual relationships for similar reasons. They see the prospect of liberation in an adult relationship, and the promise of love and being wanted. This quickly fades into the reality of control—often violent—and in some cases even being used to raise money through prostitution. A teenage boy who has left an unhappy home may initially be flattered by the interest shown in him by a stranger, but can end up in similar danger.

# Jesus and the Pharisees

We can learn much from reading what Jesus had to say about leadership in general, and more specifically about those who exercised authority in his day. In Matthew 23 we read some of Jesus' teaching given to ordinary folk. He was speaking (v. 1) to 'the crowds and to his disciples' about their spiritual leaders.

Jesus began by affirming the value of their teachings, which had been handed down from Moses, but instructed (v. 3) '...do not do what they do, for they do not practise what they preach'. Jesus saw a system which crushed men and women under heavy burdens while their leaders did nothing to help (v. 4). They were too busy revelling in their status, creating opportunities for people to honour them (vv. 5–7) and being conspicuously 'spiritual' (see also Matthew 6:1–18).

Instead of drawing others closer to God, they were effectively barring them from his Kingdom (Matthew 23:13). And it seems they weren't as close to God themselves as they liked to think (v. 13b). The religious leaders put tremendous effort into making converts, but they were converts to something which had its origins in hell rather than in heaven (v. 15).

## Misusing the scriptures

The Pharisees made complicated additions to the scriptures—so difficult to follow that only they could be trusted to give the correct interpretation. For example (Matthew 23:16), they concocted a teaching which said that if anyone were to swear 'by the temple' it wouldn't count, but if he swore 'by the gold of the temple' it would be a binding oath. Jesus saw them as 'blind guides' and 'fools', and wasn't afraid—or too 'polite'—to say so.

Whilst pretending that the scriptures were of paramount importance, the leaders failed to show true respect for them. Sometimes they adhered to the letter of the law whilst overlooking the real issues (Matthew 23:23–26; see also Matthew 12:9–12). They even interpreted the scriptures to suit their own purposes. For example, in Mark 7:8–13 Jesus took them to task for setting aside the command to honour their father and mother. They claimed that if they devoted to God what their parents might have been expecting to receive that was OK.

Jesus knew that the scriptures pointed to his coming. The teachers of the law and the Pharisees needed to lift their eyes from their meticulous scrutiny of the text in order to see the fulfilment. Jesus stated this clearly: 'You diligently study the Scriptures because you think that by them you possess eternal life. These are the Scriptures that testify about me, yet you refuse to come to me to have life' (John 5:39–40). The Pharisees knew the scriptures well, but they had become a weapon in their armoury to be used for their own purposes.

## *Corrupt religion*

A few of the religious leaders did follow Jesus but it seems that the majority were more concerned to protect their own interests. They saw him as a dangerous man and plotted to get rid of him: 'Here is this man performing many miraculous signs. If we let him go on like this, everyone will believe in him, and then the Romans will come and take away both our place and our nation' (John 11: 47–48).

The irony is that even when they were taking Jesus to Pilate, the Roman governor, to ask for him to be crucified, the Jews were careful to avoid becoming contaminated (ceremonially unclean). They stopped short of entering his palace (John 18:28), because they wanted to be able to participate in the Passover. In so doing they appeared to be scrupulous in their observance, but in reality they were demonstrating their contempt for God's law.

They probably saw themselves as above the law—they could choose to ignore the bit about bearing false witness (Matthew 26:59) because it suited their purposes, and plotting to kill someone could be excused if the someone was as inconvenient to have around as Jesus. 'We have no king but Caesar,' the chief priests shouted (John 19:15), suspending for a convenient moment their abhorrence of all things Roman—and, of course, at the same time putting to one side their allegiance to God.

Jesus saw beyond the Pharisees' impressive religiosity. He recognized their soul-destroying abuses of the ordinary folk who looked to them for leadership. In language reminiscent of John the Baptist, Jesus called them snakes and vipers. He knew that, when spiritual authority is exercised corruptly, the end pretty soon justifies the means. Control *must* be exercised—by fair means or foul. Using people, using the scriptures, using whatever comes to hand. He knew what they were capable of.

# Spiritual and sexual abuse

Today, abuse of authority comes in many forms—some shocking, some relatively minor, but none of them pleasing to or honouring to God.

## *Spiritual abuse*

The term 'spiritual abuse' is an emotive one. For many people it brings memories of horrific items in TV news broadcasts and the newspapers. Brain-washed zombies, we are told, followed their leader's decrees, and perhaps also willingly submitted to (or allowed their children to be exposed to) abhorrent sexual practices.

In recent years many have apparently unquestioningly followed cult leaders to their death, in Waco (Texas), in Rancho Santa Fe (California), and in groups belonging to the cult of the Solar Temple. In other cults the 'death' of members is by physical separation and psychological alienation, a living death as far as their rejected families are concerned. But spiritual abuse is not confined to cults and strange religions.

## *Vulnerable people*
## *need healthy relationships*

Christian groups attract vulnerable, hurting individuals. This is good, but we must make sure that they are offered what they need and not further abused or stunted in their growth. Men and women who are vulnerable because of past abuse or for any other reason need healthy relationships within which they can begin to learn how to function as mature adults. We'll be keen to introduce people to Christ, but, as part of caring for them, it may be necessary also to give some guidance on relationships and what it is appropriate to share with whom and under what circumstances. Those who spend all their time doing the rounds, telling their deepest problems to one person after another, are not usually receiving the help they need, and this approach lays them open to abuse.

Vulnerable, hurting people can be messy to deal with. Instead of supporting them as they inch their way through their difficulties, the temptation can be to opt for getting them under control. But if we say: 'Don't think that', 'You shouldn't feel that', and 'God is telling me that you ought to...' we are abusing them, crushing their spirits, not allowing them to grow.

Turning from those who are vulnerable to those who have

achieved a degree of maturity and stability: we need to ask whether the groups to which we belong encourage continuing personal growth and healthy discipleship, or whether there is a tendency for members to become rigid or increasingly passive.

## Controlling the spiritual journey of another

It is spiritually abusive for one person to seek to control the spiritual journey of another. Much that is good takes place in the context of counselling, mentoring, spiritual direction, and informal friend-to-friend guidance. Since I became a Christian thirty-five years ago, I have been blessed on countless occasions by someone older—or younger—and wiser taking time to listen, to gently question, to share from their own experience, to caution, to encourage, to suggest… My spiritual journey has been greatly enriched by such people, and I thank God for them. Many mature Christians look back with gratitude to those whom God has used to stimulate their Christian growth and to encourage them in their walk with him at key points in their lives.

But sometimes we encounter individuals who, we gradually realize, have significant unresolved personal issues which give them a need to control. They strongly advise (they may use the word 'encourage'). If others appear to be hesitating before acting on the advice, they may take the trouble to remind them that, whilst being free to take another course if they see fit, they'd be well-advised to do as suggested. The 'help' given by such folk can prove damaging to the person who seeks it—or to the person who is being given it whether or not they were seeking it!

## Failing to encourage evaluation

I believe that it is also spiritually abusive to exercise authority without encouraging people to evaluate teaching and practices for themselves. Teaching church members to question and test things feels very risky, and of course they may well use this freedom to question us not just when we're on the wrong track, but when we're on the right track too! This can lead to friction, delay and added weariness.

Some folk question absolutely everything, and oppose all change to established practices as a matter of principle—and they need encouragement to face the insecurities which lead them to act in this way. But I'd rather teach church members to use their God-given faculties, and make time for unproductive questioning, than stunt spiritual growth by turning out 'Yes-people'.

## 'A living sacrifice'

Many Christians willingly sacrifice wealth and worldly career prospects in order to serve the Lord in full-time Christian work. Others consciously decline career advancement because they recognize that taking greater responsibility at work would involve a greater commitment than they are willing to make in that direction. They choose to accept lower pay and reduced prospects because they believe the Lord is calling them to devote a significant amount of time to youth work, counselling, or a preaching ministry, which they would be unable to sustain if they were having to travel a lot for work, or always needing to stay late at the office for management meetings.

In Romans 12 (vv. 1–2), after urging his readers to present their bodies as 'living sacrifices', Paul goes on to exhort them not to allow the world to impose its pattern on them. Rather, they should allow God to transform them by the renewing of their minds, in order that they might be able to discern God's will. God does sometimes call us to make difficult decisions which are contrary to the flow of the rest of the world. Often it's only with hindsight that we can see that what felt like a loss, or a crazy choice, has been the doorway to great blessing. God is delighted when we choose to trust him and take a step of faith. The result is that we grow closer to him, and our faith and understanding of his ways and purposes is strengthened.

Problems arise, however, when leaders look to church members to make similar sacrifices which feel compulsory rather than voluntary. I have heard of people being told by their church leaders to give up their job, move to a new area, or decline the offer of a university place when they themselves had no sense that this was God's will. They were expected to obey their leaders' instructions, regardless of their own misgivings. (Perhaps they knew from past experience that their leaders could not cope with having their word questioned.)

They were being asked to obey men rather than God. This is dangerous. Church leaders often have valuable experience of discerning the Lord's will, and on many occasions I have benefited from the wise counsel of ministers I have known, but they have usually come alongside me in the process of seeking to know the right way for myself. They have not told me what I ought to be doing and expected me to jump to it unquestioningly.

## *Abuse of goodwill*

It is perhaps easier to see the dangers of trying to impose a major sacrifice on someone else than to spot a climate in which daily minor sacrifices are extracted from put-upon volunteers. Sometimes problems develop as a result of misunderstandings, or because, when asking for a volunteer, the nature of the job to be done has been only vaguely communicated. I know too many willing Christians who have offered to help with what sounded like a minor matter, only to find themselves left in sole charge of a major project. If folk are inveigled into Christian service which demands more than they feel able to commit, and then see it through only because there seems to be no way out, this does not honour God or serve his purposes. Ultimately, it is the responsibility of the person or people in leadership both to clarify expectations, and to lovingly release any volunteer who realizes belatedly that the job is not for them after all.

It should be a matter of shame that the working conditions for those employed in many churches and Christian organizations are such that they would not be tolerated elsewhere. Some are even against the law, but are suffered 'in order not to hold back the Lord's work'. Those in authority will be answerable to the Lord for the way they have treated their employees and volunteer workers. The way we treat those who work for us, indeed the way we treat all those whose voice is less powerful and influential than ours, is a mirror to our values and priorities. We need an integrated spirituality which influences our Monday to Saturday relationships as well as the way we preach or worship on Sundays.

## Sexual abuse

I don't propose to spend time explaining why it's an abuse of authority for church leaders to use members of their flock—however willing they may be—for sexual gratification. I hope that it's self-evident that in any relationship in which there is an imbalance of power (such as teacher-pupil, doctor-patient, counsellor-client, leader-led) the person with the authority is the one who is responsible for ensuring that the relationship stays within accepted boundaries; sexual activity of any sort is outside these boundaries, and constitutes an abuse of authority, regardless of who apparently initiated it. Should a close friendship appear to be developing between an unmarried church leader and an unmarried church member, the leader should make another leader aware of it at an early stage, and ask them to assume pastoral responsibility for the church member. This may sound a harsh thing to say, as developing relationships can be very fragile and a desire to maintain privacy is understandable, but an unwillingness to disclose such a relationship to one other leader must raise a question mark.

It is vital for church leaders to accept that, if unacceptable behaviour of any sort comes to light, it's abusive to minimize the importance of what has happened, or to suggest no action in order to avoid the risk of unfavourable publicity. It's only too easy for a person who has been abused by someone in a position of power to be further abused by other leaders who are primarily interested in their 'window display' or 'keeping the peace'. This does not honour God.

# The use and abuse of scripture

Many churches emphasize the importance of the Bible. However, today as well as in Jesus' day, the scriptures may be abused as well as used. It is tempting to assume that if the Bible is being quoted all must be well, but this is not so. It is worth noting in passing that Satan himself tried to use the scriptures when he tempted Jesus in the wilderness (Matthew 4:1–11).

## How is scripture being used?

When leaders quote from the Bible, are they doing so in order to encourage everyone to read it for themselves, thereby feeding their understanding and developing their Christian maturity, or is it done mainly for the purpose of control—bringing troublesome individuals or groups into line? It is possible to use passages of scripture manipulatively, for example: reading out Philippians 2:2, in which Paul urges the Christians to 'make my joy complete by being like-minded, having the same love, being one in spirit and purpose' when about to discuss a contentious issue. Done in a manipulative way, this could pressurize people into saying they agree with whatever is suggested, for fear of 'going against scripture'. In a group where the leaders are very controlling, and being a 'Yes-person' is seen as a Christian virtue, it would take a strong character to raise objections having heard such a heart-felt plea from the scriptures.

Similarly, verses about not sitting in judgment on one another can be used to short-circuit any criticism. After all, if you're saying I'm wrong, you're judging me—so you're the one who's at fault! As with the example above, the problem lies not with the scripture verses, but with the prevailing atmosphere in the group which inclines people both to use and to hear the words in a distorted way.

Some use the Bible as an armoury of bullets, which can be fired off from time to time to underline the leaders' authority and to prove that they are right. The Bible is not a collection of proof texts; it is composed of separate books, each of which has a beginning, a middle, and an end. Preachers and leaders who make a habit of pulling out single verses which suit their particular emphasis of the moment are in danger of concealing more than they reveal. Some cults use this method to hook the attention of outsiders and to give their teaching an appearance of mainstream respectability. We need to make sure that we 'live as children of light' (Ephesians 5:8) and avoid using questionable means to achieve what we see as worthy ends.

## Single-verse-proofs

A card tucked in the back of the Bible (or, with practice, a memorized equivalent) may be relied on for one-verse answers to common questions or dilemmas. It's possible to find an unhealthy pseudo-security in knowing an answer to every possible question —having everything under control and every eventuality covered. Would that life were that simple! Few questions of any importance can be answered briefly without any loose ends.

I have nothing against jottings to aid fallible memories, but the single-verse-proof method often fails to convey *understanding*. It can also leave the hearers in ignorance of the surrounding verses, and of other passages of scripture on the same subject. Such useful lists are sometimes photocopied and handed out. When it becomes obvious that someone has unquestioningly adopted a second-hand list of answers, I start to worry.

As a teenager I attended the preparatory training for a Billy Graham Mission, which included memorizing key verses of the Bible with their references. I have no quarrel with those who encourage Christians to be familiar with key verses, especially if they also memorize where to find them. This is clearly appropriate in a mission training context, and many Christians can testify to the blessing they received from a single verse of scripture which came to mind in a time of crisis. But this is the 'emergency rations' approach to scripture, and not a route to good long-term health. If, thirty years on, all I knew about the book of Romans was 3:23 and 8:1, I would be greatly impoverished! These two verses which I learned at the training sessions in my teens were welcome landmarks in unknown and formidable territory; now they are familiar features in a well-known landscape.

## *'The Bible says...' Or does it?*

Teaching on the subject of spiritual abuse on an advanced course for Christian counsellors, I produced a selection of things which 'the Bible says', and asked for comments. How would *you* respond if I assured you that, for example, 'the Bible says that women must submit to men', or 'the Bible says Christians must give ten per cent of their income to the church'?

Most of the participants on the course were Christians with many years of church-going behind them, but many clearly had difficulty in distinguishing my distortions from what the Bible actually says. The following year, teaching on the same course but working with a group from a different range of church back-grounds, I was pleased to find that people were better able to spot what was wrong.

In fact, the Bible says (Ephesians 5:22) 'Wives, submit to your husbands'. Although the Greek words for wives/husbands can also be translated women/men, the context makes it clear that the passage is speaking about those who are married. Incidentally, the previous verse says 'Submit to one another out of reverence for Christ'. Why do discussions on this topic so often begin with verse 22?

Nowhere does the New Testament give a formula for working out financial giving for Christians. The figure of ten per cent (a tithe) is taken from the Old Testament, although a detailed study will reveal that in practice more than ten per cent was given to God. A prayer used in the Church of England at the time of the offering is based on 1 Chronicles 29:14 which says: 'Everything comes from you, and we have given you only what comes from your hand.' We are to be good stewards of all that God has given us, and we shall be answerable to him for what we do with it all— not just what proportion of our income we put in the collection plate, and not just what we do with our money.

Problems can arise in fellowships where the leaders act as if there were no distinction between what is to be given to God and what is to be given to the church. Their members are exhorted to tithe their income, and it is not seen as acceptable to give to God's work other than through the fellowship to which they belong. I see this as an abuse of authority. In addition, there are dangers in the 'set formula' approach. Firstly, some may feel that, once they have given the church their cut, God will take no interest in what they do with the rest. Secondly, in applying one formula to everyone, individuals will be more inclined to give as they are told rather than as the Lord leads. He might be asking some to give far more than ten per cent of their income! He will certainly be paying rather more attention to the heart of each giver than to the arithmetic calculations.

## Distortions of the truth

It saddens me that from time to time in counselling I come across Christians with deeply held beliefs which they believe to be based on scripture, but which are in fact distortions of biblical truth. Sometimes they have spent many uneasy years doing mental gymnastics, trying to align heart and mind with what they have been told to believe. It may have affected their ability to relate to God himself, if the teaching has given a distorted picture of his nature.

Women have shared with me their concern that they've been told that the scriptures sanction rape within marriage. The passage used in justification comes from 1 Corinthians 7, although the women have not been given chapter and verse—only 'the Bible says...' It does speak of marital duty, but the emphasis is on mutuality: 'The wife's body does not belong to her alone but also to her husband. In the same way, the husband's body does not belong to him alone but also to his wife. Do not deprive each other except by mutual consent...' (1 Corinthians 7:4–5)

It requires a very bizarre reading of the passage to see this as sanctioning sexual violence. This interpretation also flies in the face of other passages of scripture (the single-verse-proof technique again) such as the end of Ephesians 5 in which husbands are told to love their wives 'as Christ loved the church' (verse 25) and 'as their own bodies' (verse 28). The Greek word here translated love is not erotic sexual love. It is *agape* love, unconditional gift love, the sort of love God has for us. Would such love even contemplate rape—let alone seeking to use the scriptures in justification for such an act?

## Free to get it wrong

All Christians need to be encouraged to read the Bible for themselves, rather than relying on other people's hand-me-down quotes and half-remembered ideas. In Acts 17:11 the writer commends the Bereans, who 'received the message with great eagerness and examined the Scriptures every day to see if what Paul said was true.' At a recent confirmation service I attended, the bishop encouraged those being confirmed to bring Bibles with them to church so that they could follow the passages being referred to and check out what the preacher was saying. Leaders who use the Bible as a way of keeping control of their church will be less inclined to encourage individuals to search the scriptures for themselves. They would have come down hard on the Bereans' check-it-out-for-myself approach!

Encouraging people to study the Bible, to mull it over, read commentaries about it, question the origins of established interpretations, and to draw their own conclusions—even if they are wrong—is the best prevention of spiritual abuse I know. God speaks to those who earnestly seek him. If someone gets the wrong end of the stick by studying and seeking to understand, they will probably in time move to a position of greater understanding. If someone believes a mistaken interpretation of scripture because they have been told to do so, they may lack the freedom to examine their belief and realize that they are in error.

# Healthy discipling

Having said that it's important to allow church members the freedom to question established interpretations and even to make mistakes, it's also important to offer everyone access to the sort of skills and guidance which will help them to grow in faith and understanding. Young people, and new Christians of any age, need to be given clear instruction from the scriptures on the basics of Christian belief. They need to be guided through landmark doctrines to help them get their bearings. It's also helpful for new Christians to be shown a well-signposted path of discipleship, to help them get started on their journey, and to be introduced to more experienced fellow-travellers who will be walking with them.

This degree of guidance is appropriate for that stage of their Christian lives, just as receiving milk at regular intervals, and being spoon-fed mushed-up food were appropriate for us all in the early stages of our physical lives. But we don't expect mature healthy adults to be fed like babies, or to have similar nutritional needs, and the same is true in spiritual terms. When babies move on to solid food and start to want to feed themselves it can be trying for all concerned, but no one would attempt to keep them sitting in a high chair and spoon-fed on mush for ever in order to avoid the difficulties of the transition to a full adult diet!

## *Appropriate nourishment*

Many churches appear to lack a real understanding of the varying needs of their members. In the 1990s, the phenomenal growth of the Willow Creek church in Illinois, USA, through seeker-friendly services, raised awareness of the needs of those who are interested in Christianity yet know little or nothing about it. Many churches have followed their example and held 'Seeker Services', in which people are not asked to recite creeds or sing hymns which they don't believe. Instead they are presented with the gospel, probably using drama and music in addition to speaking in plain English, and invited to consider their response.

The internationally known Alpha courses (devised by Holy Trinity, Brompton, and published by Kingsway) emphasize the need for a planned programme of teaching which explains key doctrines and encourages the asking of questions. For this reason, Alpha courses are also ideal for individuals who have attended church for many years, but have laboured under the impression that asking questions is a sign of lack of commitment or in some way disloyal.

Some see Alpha courses as too closely linked with one strand of spirituality, or stressing a particular doctrinal stance. It would be difficult for any course to be all things to all people, but, given the experience in my home town where churches with widely differing emphases and doctrinal positions have successfully used the courses, I don't believe that the difficulties are insuperable. In my church some sessions or parts of sessions are taught without using the official videos, which can be used selectively.

Another benefit of Alpha courses is that they provide opportunities for training up new leaders to take responsibility. The material provided enables them to draw on the experience of others as appropriate, and to use their own skills and knowledge to the full without feeling abandoned. No doubt we have all learned valuable lessons through being extended beyond what we thought was possible, but dropping someone in the deep end as a teacher of others, and leaving them to flounder without support, can be abusive—*and* a less-than-ideal learning experience for those they are expected to teach.

## *Fight the spiritual flab!*

What about those who have been Christians for decades, yet continue to use the same Bible reading notes as they used as a new Christian, or are still silently sitting through weekly Bible study groups—some of which are taken by trainee ministers now less than half their age? In 1 Corinthians 3:2 Paul expresses disappointment that he had felt it necessary to feed his readers with milk, rather than more substantial spiritual food. The same complaint is made by the writer to the Hebrews, who chided his readers for their lack of progress from spiritual baby food to real meat, and was clearly disappointed that those who should have been able to teach others were still at the nursery stage (Hebrews 5:11–14).

It is wasteful and abusive for Christians to go on receiving the spiritual equivalent of milk or spoon-fed mushy baby food when they are needing to get their teeth into some meat—and do a bit of chewing for themselves! If we don't use our minds and our critical faculties, and neglect to chew over God's Word and to extract the nourishment we need, we'll end up flabby Christians without spiritual teeth. If we quench our congregation's thirst with spiritual milk shakes and fizzy drinks, and feed them only bite-sized melt-in-the-mouth snacks, they'll end up malnourished, and ill-prepared to face the challenges to their faith which they are bound to encounter in everyday life.

We need to bear in mind, however, that some church members may have grown up believing that it is wrong—or dangerous—to even appear to question authority of any sort. They will find it hard to progress from the baby-food stage of pre-digested beliefs. They may become anxious if encouraged to chew over a Bible passage for themselves. They will prefer to be told what it says—that's safer. It would be easy to dismiss such people as weak or disinterested, when in fact they may have been kept forcibly at the nursery stage by others. Rigid or oppressive parenting and schooling may have combined with an authoritarian religion to retard their development. Their current church can only be part of the process of healing if the climate is such that it is *genuinely* safe for them to ask questions and develop their critical faculties. If it is, in time they will grow and mature, but it will take time.

## *Opportunities for exercise*

In my own church fellowship we have for some years encouraged house groups to take occasional responsibility for the Sunday evening service. Members of a group will plan the service and its theme, choose appropriate hymns and songs, lead, read lessons, preach, lead in prayer, and play as much of the music as the group can manage. Individuals can find it quite nerve-wracking if they've never done anything like this before, but, surrounded by their friends in the group, they take their courage in both hands and have a go—often with amazing results!

I recall being at one such service, and heard a lady read who had never done so before. She had a beautiful speaking voice, and read clearly, with understanding. When the house group of which I am a member took a service, a book designer called John preached for the first time. The scriptures and thoughts he shared with us in preparation were an encouragement to me, and he constructed them into a sermon which we found helpful. John is on the list of occasional preachers, and is exploring a call to the ordained ministry.

## *Building faith*

When people are given this sort of opportunity, it encourages them to move on in their Christian lives, and to chew over the scriptures with a new urgency, whether in order to read with understanding or to preach. Putting a service together or choosing hymns and songs to go with a particular theme usually increases people's awareness of what it means to worship, and can draw them much closer to God—*and* exercise their faith as they contemplate doing something for the first time, wondering if the congregation will be distracted by the sound of their knees knocking!

Yes, indivduals must to be able to say 'No' when asked to participate. Leaders will need to take care to allocate responsibility in accordance with people's gifts, to provide support in preparation if required, and to follow up as necessary. But don't let fear of some rough edges or a less than perfect performance prevent a much-needed growing experience.

If we're in leadership, we may have to answer to God for keeping church members in an infantile state when we should have been encouraging them to grow, develop, train and move towards maturity. How many ministers would prefer to forget the first sermon they preached, or the first service they led? Can you remember who it was who trusted you to try again when you faltered over your first reading or sermon? Was there someone who encouraged you by telling you that God had blessed them through your words when you were sure that you'd been too nervous to make sense? Thank God for such men and women!

## Individually God's children

Those whose leadership honours God and is a blessing to others have usually grasped the vital truth that the people they lead are all individually God's children and therefore have the same free access to the Father as they do; God's children are not obliged to relate to him only through a third party. In his letter to the Romans (Romans 8:16) Paul writes: 'The Spirit himself testifies with our spirit that we are God's children.' This verse comes from a very profound passage in which he urges his readers to lay hold of their amazing inheritance in Christ, and to enter fully into their relationship with '*Abba*, Father'.

Reading Paul's epistles, we can have little doubt that he was a strong leader. He urged everyone to respect those who had authority over them in the Lord (1 Thessalonians 5:12), but he repeatedly used his authority as an apostle to point people away from human leaders to Christ. He painted some exciting wordpictures (for example, in 1 Corinthians 12:12–31) about the necessary inter-relatedness of believers in the body of Christ. But he never lost sight of the need for people also to respond individually and personally to the call of God upon their lives.

Christians who do not hear the inner testimony of God's Spirit that they are children of God, and lack a sense of *Abba* Father's face being turned lovingly towards them, are not only impoverished: they are very vulnerable to abuse. Nowhere is this more apparent than in the context of prayer ministry.

# Prayer ministry

The past ten years have seen a dramatic rise in the number of opportunities for receiving the laying on of hands for healing or prayer ministry of one sort or another. This happens both in churches and at specialist centres, such as the Old Rectory, Crowhurst, not far from where I live. My own experiences of being prayed for at Crowhurst have all been positive, and I am delighted that prayer ministry is now more widely available, but I am also concerned that this gives opportunities for vulnerable hurting individuals to be further wounded.

Even the most ordinary man or woman becomes invested with authority in the eyes of others when they take on a prayer ministry. Thus, when someone comes to ask for prayer, the relationship is likely to be on an unequal footing from the outset. This means that everything which is done, said or implied by the person ministering will carry extra significance and weight for the person seeking help.

This brings tremendous responsibility, and I believe that training for prayer ministry needs to include teaching on how not to abuse vulnerable people. It also needs to include clear examples of what 'abuse' means.

## 'That's better, isn't it?'

Many socially acceptable passing comments (such as 'That's better, isn't it?') are potentially abusive in the context of prayer ministry. Careless use of phrases which close a session by implying a satisfactory end result—without asking the person being prayed for how they feel—may seem pretty harmless compared with more devastating forms of abuse, but if someone has opened their heart to others in order that they might be prayed for, and feels no better (or even worse) at the end of the prayer time, they'll be very vulnerable.

Sometimes few words are said, and the praying is done in silence. The implicit assumption at the end of the time of prayer is that the matter has been brought before God and that he will act as he sees fit. Where the style is more interactive, it can sometimes be helpful to ask—gently, and without looking as if only one answer will do—how the person is feeling. If they feel better already, then we'll be able to give thanks to God. If they don't, we can encourage them to be open about their feelings before God, and perhaps pray a 'holding' prayer, asking God to enfold them in his love until such a time as they do feel better, or are able to come for further prayer.

I believe that anything which encourages people to say they believe things they're not sure about, or to pretend to feel emotions which they don't feel—and which whitewashes over the emotions they *do* feel in the context of prayer ministry—is abusive.

## Encouraging real faith

Being prayed for can be a tremendous faith-raising experience. But this will only prove beneficial and give glory to God if it's raising genuine faith, rather than an appearance of faith designed to please those who have been doing the praying, and to give them the perfect end result which they appear to need. Faked spiritual experiences do not build faith. They undermine it, and they're abusive if initiated by others rather than self-generated.

I remember many years ago attending a course on praying for people at a respected healing mission. At the end of the course, we had a short service after which we asked the Lord to minister to us. Members of staff moved amongst us, praying for individuals. Several fell to the floor and lay prostrate. A lady came to pray for me. I suddenly became aware that her hand was on my back, and her fingers were digging hard into my flesh, with a pressure that was clearly designed to send me towards the floor. I began to wonder if that was what had happened to the others who were already there!

In those days I was unfamiliar with healing prayer, and very uncertain about what to expect. I knew that what was happening was not of God, so I resisted it, but I lacked the courage to say anything. If such an experience happened to me today, I hope I would say in an assertive voice, 'Please stop digging your fingers into me' or something similar. Today, I find that being open about this sort of experience in conversation or teaching releases a flood of tales from others who have felt pressurized to perform to order.

## *Encouraging participation*

Many who come to be prayed for will want to assume a passive role, to roll over and play dead while something magical is done to them. Some will be looking for a cure for a malaise which is at least in part of their own making—for example, stress due to an unwillingness to say 'No'. Many have a strong preference for a cure which is painless and requires no effort from them. And could it, please, be instantaneous? This can mistakenly be seen as a manifestation of great faith! It needs to be challenged—gently but firmly.

Whatever the person's needs or approach, it is vital that what happens in the time of prayer ministry engages, as far as is possible, with their thoughts, feelings and will, and draws them closer to God, rather than leaving them feeling more distant from him. When I was learning to pray in this way, I was taught to ask people from time to time if they were aware of anything happening—not in such a way as to pressurize them to invent something for my benefit, but to encourage them to remain active in the process. They needed to feel free to share any pictures or words that came into their mind, as well as any physical sensations.

On occasions, people have shared pictures which have closely tallied with words which I had felt God was giving to me as I prayed. If I had rushed in and given my 'word from the Lord' without asking them what was happening first, they might not have shared their picture. They might even have been left feeling mightily impressed with how God spoke to me, and disappointed that God never said that sort of thing to them!

I was instructed to offer possible insights from the Lord as just that: 'possible insights'—not holy writ. We need to offer 'words from the Lord' as I was taught to offer sugar lumps to a horse: on an open palm, so that they can be looked at and picked up if required. Don't shove them forcibly down the throat! This is particularly important when the insights (presumed to be from the Lord) are much less palatable than sugar lumps, and much more difficult to swallow. The tendency can be to give that sort of insight an extra hard push to make sure that it can't be refused!

## Being aware of
## our own feelings and motives

Those who work as counsellors are taught to monitor what is going on within themselves as they counsel others. To some extent this can be done through honest self-examination, but it is best undertaken in a supervisory relationship. The Association of Christian Counsellors decided early on in its existence that it would not accredit anyone who was not in regular supervision, and I think that this has been a decision of vital importance. I would welcome a climate in which it is considered normal to have similar supervisory arrangements for those who regularly pray for others. Within such relationships they can be prompted to answer the sort of questions which need to be asked, such as:

- For whose benefit am I doing this?

- How strong is my need for success?

- How much do I need approval—from those for whom I pray, and from those who see me in this role?

- Do I feel the need to know exactly what God is saying in every situation?

- Is this ministry becoming so important to me that it is taking up time which should be committed elsewhere?

- Do I feel close to God when I'm *not* praying for people?

## Learning about listening
## —and the pitfalls

In my home church we ran a listening skills course, for those involved with prayer ministry and other pastoral work, and for anyone else interested in participating. Everyone was surprised to learn just how much of our communication is non-verbal. They quickly caught on to the fact that it's pointless saying 'I'm listening' if our body language is saying the opposite.

During the course we encouraged participants to use their own past and present experience of being listened to, or *not* being listened to, to learn how it felt to be handled in different ways. In addition to stimulating a more sensitive approach to others, this also encouraged them to develop a healthily critical attitude towards what was being done to them. In the final session we raised the subject of being prayed for, and two ladies shared how they had separately been prayed for in ways which left them feeling uncomfortable. Both had felt 'bad' for not liking what had happened, and guilty for not feeling grateful. To broach this subject we had used the story about Lucy's ministry at the hands of Pastor Bill, which is fictional but unfortunately close enough to what can happen to be recognizable.

*Lucy, the wife of one of the deacons, had arrived late for the service. She sat on her own at the back, looking somewhat preoccupied. At the end of the service, Pastor Bill used the words of Jesus in Matthew 11, verse 28, 'Come to me, all you who are weary and burdened, and I will give you rest...' to invite all who were bearing burdens to come forward for prayer.*

*At first, Lucy stayed put, but, as the church building emptied, she went forward and sat in the front row. When her turn came, Pastor Bill came and stood in front of her and asked her what her need was. She burst into tears, and, for some considerable time, was unable to speak.*

*Lucy eventually managed to compose herself sufficiently to blurt out: 'Pastor, I'm so afraid.'*

*Pastor Bill opened his Bible. 'As a mature Christian,' he said, 'I'm sure you know, Lucy, that 1 John 4 verse 18 says: "Perfect love drives out fear". I'm going to pray that God will make the truth of that verse a reality for you right now.' Pastor Bill put his left hand on Lucy's shoulder, lifted his right hand to heaven, and prayed as he had said.*

*'That's better, isn't it?' he beamed at Lucy, who struggled to give a weak smile in reply. 'Now, if you'll excuse me, I must be going as I have something really important to attend to.' And with that, he left.*

We asked everyone to decide what they thought Lucy's problem was. (She goes to Bill's church; is a deacon's wife; who knows!) When asked what Lucy needed, they agreed that first and foremost she needed to be heard. But what did she receive? We wondered aloud together what Pastor Bill might have learned if a similar course had been run in his church, but we weren't convinced that he'd have been keen to attend.

Sadly, some see the teaching of listening skills and reminders about body language as unnecessary in the context of Christian ministry, because, they say, the Holy Spirit will come alongside and bring all the wisdom and skill of the wonderful counsellor. I am afraid that it requires considerable denial to make this assertion! Such denial may sound spiritual enough, but can actually signal a disabling fear of loss of control.

The gracious Holy Spirit works miracles, and uses fallible and inadequate human beings as his channels. The problem comes when the imperfect channels start to see themselves as perfect (well, *close* to perfect—expert perhaps?) and rely on well-worn techniques, magical phrases, spiritual mystique, an authoritative manner and a loud voice to bring about what only God himself can achieve. If they *do* sense that all is not well, the temptation can be to turn up the volume or the spiritual temperature, and to focus more firmly on the result which they require to notch up another 'success'. Once the focus shifts from the Lord to 'the required result', abuse of vulnerable people is often not far down the road.

# How did Jesus deal with people?

Just as we can learn from Jesus' attitude to the leaders of his day, we can also benefit from studying how he—a leader—behaved towards others. 'Walk with me and work with me—watch how I do it,' Jesus said (Matthew 11:29, *The Message*); let's see how we can apply this principle with regard to our leadership responsibilities. (Study 6 at the end of the book provides additional suggestions.)

## *Servant leadership*

Jesus wasn't afraid to give a strong lead from an up-front position, but undergirding all he did and said was his conviction that he had come to serve: 'Whoever wants to become great among you must be your servant, and whoever wants to be first must be your slave—just as the Son of Man did not come to be served, but to serve, and to give his life as a ransom for many' (Matthew 20: 26–28).

Jesus' actions backed up his words. His washing of the disciples' feet (John 13:5) is an oft-quoted demonstration of his servant-leadership, but I believe that day by day his manner of dealing with individuals would have been distinctively different from that of the other religious leaders of the time.

While others sought to associate with the right people in order to emphasize their importance, Jesus was happy to be seen with anyone—fisherman, tax collector, Samaritan woman with a bad reputation, prostitute, leper... He was not averse to being seen with the rich and influential either: he looked with love on the rich young man (Mark 10:21); he was willing to go to the home of a Roman centurion to heal his servant (Matthew 8:7); he accepted an invitation to a meal at the house of Simon the pharisee (Luke 7:36); and after his death he rested briefly in the grave of a rich man (Matthew 27:60). But he did not crave the company of important people, as some seem to do.

Jesus was prepared to use his authority to confront powerful individuals and groups when necessary, yet he dealt very gently with those who were without power or position, such as the children (Matthew 19:13–15), and those whom others were willing to abuse, such as the woman taken in adultery (John 8:3–11). We do well to question whose example we are following if we find ourselves favouring the powerful to the detriment of those without a voice.

The writer to the Hebrews (4:15–16) emphasized that although Jesus himself was sinless, he was tempted 'in every way, just as we are', and is able to sympathize with our weaknesses. When others were prepared to lay down the law, Jesus said, 'Go now and leave your life of sin' (John 8:11). In no way was he soft on sin—but he had great compassion for the sinner. Fellow Christians who *are* sinners can sometimes be less clear about the necessity to flee from all sin and much harder on anyone caught sinning!

## Meeting people where they were

Reading the gospels, we see that Jesus met with men and women where they were, took them as he found them, and offered them the opportunity to move on—but only offered, mind you: the choice was theirs. He often dealt with people as individuals or in small groups. His words revealed understanding of where they were coming from, and what their real needs were.

Jesus taught using stories about scattering seed, weeds growing up with the crops, losing sheep and coins, building houses, hiring workers, being in debt... the variegated threads of contemporary lives. He called himself the good shepherd, the door to the sheepfold, the vine, the bread of life, living water... Rather than using a specialized vocabulary or grand titles to distance himself from ordinary folk, Jesus came right alongside. He spoke of spiritual mysteries in common-or-garden language, thus, I believe, indicating that they really were meant to be a part of everyday life for everyone. He broke the stranglehold of the professional religious types who specialized in making the things of God inaccessible to all but a favoured few. Is this our approach?

Jesus challenged people at the points where he knew they needed to grow, but without ridiculing or humiliating. Above all, he shared his life with them, and allowed them to learn by seeing the way he behaved, and the way he related to the Father. He didn't have to say: 'Do as I say, not as I do', because there was no gap between his teaching and his manner of life. Later, Paul urged the Corinthian Christians: 'Follow my example, as I follow the example of Christ' (1 Corinthians 11:1). Peter wrote to those with responsibility in the early church: 'Be shepherds of God's flock that is under your care... not lording it over those entrusted to you, but being examples to the flock. And when the Chief Shepherd appears, you will receive the crown of glory that will never fade away' (1 Peter 5:2–4).

When at the end of our lives we meet Jesus, the Chief Shepherd, we'll be answerable for the way we've exercised whatever authority we've been given—in the church, but also at home, at work, in all our dealings with others. Let's ask the Lord to make us aware of any ways in which we've been misusing our authority—or failing to use it for good, as he intends.

# Focus point

**'What's my spiritual diet like? Is it appropriate?'**

Milk and mush? Meat and solid food needing chewing? Or fast-food snacks—the spiritual equivalent of crisps and pop? If appropriate, also ask yourself: **'What am I feeding to others? Am I encouraging them to develop their spiritual teeth?'**

**'Do the encounters I have with people encourage them to draw closer to God?'**

**'Or does my bearing, or my use of religious language, simply leave them feeling impressed by *my* closeness to God?'**

Servant leadership? Meditate on Jesus' words in Mark 10:42–45, and his demonstration of servant leadership in John 13:1–17. You could perhaps read these passages daily for a short period, but in any case try to carry them in your mind for a while and see how they speak into your situation.

# Compassion—the real thing or a cheap imitation?

## 2 Corinthians 1:3—4

*Praise be to the God and Father of our Lord Jesus Christ, the Father of compassion and the God of all comfort, who comforts us in all our troubles, so that we can comfort those in any trouble with the comfort we ourselves have received from God.*

Compassion is part of God's nature. In Psalm 145:8–9, David tells us that 'the Lord is gracious and compassionate, slow to anger and rich in love... he has compassion on all he has made.' Paul refers to God as 'the Father of compassion' (2 Corinthians 1:3).

When Jesus saw the crowds who followed him or waited to catch sight of him, 'he had compassion on them, because they were harassed and helpless, like sheep without a shepherd' (Matthew 9:36). His compassion led him to ask the disciples to find food for those who had been listening to his teaching, lest they collapse on the way home (Matthew 15:32). On other occasions, Jesus' compassion stirred him to heal people (Matthew 20:34; Mark 1:41; Luke 7:13). After telling the stories about the joy in heaven when a lost sinner returns to God (Luke 15:1–10), Jesus told the parable of the prodigal son. While the son was still some way from home, his father saw him in the distance and ran out to meet him, 'filled with compassion for him' (Luke 15:20). By his life and by his teaching, Jesus shows us that God is indeed compassionate.

Given our calling to follow Christ and to be like him, compassion is not an optional extra for us. It's worth noting that Zechariah 7:8–12 implies that one of the things which makes our slow-to-anger God 'very angry' is failure to show compassion.

## So what is compassion?

The original documents of the Bible weren't written in English, so we're working with translations of Hebrew and Greek words, and different translators have at different times translated the same *original* words by different English words. This means that whilst in one English version we'll find the word 'compassion', in another we'll find the word 'pity' or 'mercy'.

Luke 10:33 in the New International Version, says that the good Samaritan 'took pity on' the wounded traveller, but someone using a King James Bible or the Revised Standard Version would read that he 'had compassion' on him. The Amplified Bible says that he was 'moved with pity and sympathy' for him.

Unfortunately, none of these English words really does justice to the original Hebrew and Greek words. The nearest I can get is to use a modern slang expression, and say that compassion is gut-wrenching. When the Hebrews and the Greeks talked about compassion they used words derived from the words they used for bowels; they saw the bowels as the seat of their emotions. If we're British, we'll probably prefer to say that our heart goes out to someone, or that a situation is heart-rending, rather than referring to our bowels, but the sense is the same—of a physical stirring, a sensation that touches our inner being and can't just be brushed away.

In the New Testament, the references to Jesus having compassion are almost without exception in the context of his being moved to *action*. At the end of the story of the good Samaritan, Jesus told the legal expert to 'go and do likewise'. God expects our compassion to move us to action. We need to hold on to this sense of what the word compassion really means, because our English words have become almost devalued by misuse. We've lost the impact of words like pity and sympathy, which can now be used to mean feeling sorry for someone, or understanding that they're having a bad patch.

## *It's your job to keep me happy!*

Many people seem to think that a compassionate person is one who goes along with another's wishes, whatever they happen to be. A doctor visits a patient who has been housebound for years with incurable illness. 'I'm in such pain, doctor. Can't you give me an injection so that I just go to sleep and never wake up?' A teenage girl comes to see her GP. He does a pregnancy test and finds it's positive. She's in her last year at school, and has a provisional place at university. Her GP is a compassionate, caring man. What course of action does he recommend?

I'm just glad I don't have to take that sort of decision any more. May I encourage you to pray for those who do? They need to be able to show *real* compassion—the sort of compassion that God has for us—not the counterfeit that masquerades as compassion, which really amounts to little more than doing whatever anyone asks in order to keep them happy.

## *Drop everything and come running!*

Another mistaken view is that a truly compassionate person is always ready to drop whatever they're doing and respond immediately to a request for help. Yes, there are genuine emergencies which require instant action, but in many cases it would be better to finish dealing with the job in hand before starting something else. Where the job in hand is an activity being shared with our family, it's important to recognize the significance of abandoning it in favour of someone else's needs. In effect, we are saying that what we are doing with the family is less urgent than that which the other person needs or wants us to do.

If dropping everything in order to help someone else is a frequent occurrence, and the family activities which are interrupted are seldom resumed and rarely if ever given priority, the family members may be left feeling that there's always someone more important. It's no good saying, 'Oh—but of course they're not more *important*, its just that their needs are more *urgent*.' Actions speak louder than words, and people will, over time, form their own impressions, whatever words are being said, and however fervently they are being uttered.

In any case, compassion can be shown in a variety of ways—not just by rushing to the rescue. Sometimes folk are grateful for an opportunity to think aloud about their problems and express their feelings. They won't necessarily welcome Sir Galahad on a white charger if what they actually needed was the offer of a listening ear.

## Preventative care

In some cases, problems are less urgent than people sincerely believe them to be. When I was working in General Practice I often used to see parents who had brought their child to the surgery as an emergency because they were very worried about them. Sometimes they were right to be worried, and immediate treatment prevented a serious condition becoming much worse. More often, though, it was inexperience and fear of the unknown which had generated the 'emergency'.

At the end of a long surgery it was easy to be dismissive of yet another unnecessary parental panic, but I always tried to use the opportunity constructively. I took time to explain to the parents that, while I understood their concern, the child's condition was not as serious as they had thought. By spending a minute or two talking through their child's symptoms, and telling them what to watch for in the future so that they could spot a real emergency more easily, I hope I reduced their anxiety and helped them cope with future illnesses.

The same preventative approach can be helpful in pastoral care emergencies, if people are genuinely alarmed but willing to learn how to cope better. Rushing out to help at the first sign of a minor problem can squash coping skills, and encourage people to call us rather than think things through for themselves. More generally, we need to encourage others to learn to reflect on their options, and to ask their heavenly Father for wisdom and all the resources he longs to provide, rather than seeing us as the answer.

## Agape-*love*

Compassion needs to go hand in hand with the sort of love God has for us. In the New Testament the Greek word for this kind of love is *agape*. *Agape*-love is part of the fruit of the Spirit (Galatians 5:22–23), which is the result of the character of Christ being formed in us by the working of the Holy Spirit. It's not just an optional extra for really keen Christians! God is love—*agape*-love—and *all* his children need to reflect their Father's nature.

It's called *agape*-love to distinguish it from the other kinds of love—for example, erotic love. Erotic love is a need-love—a love which drives towards fulfilment. *Agape*-love is a gift-love, which loves without any consideration of our own fulfilment or benefit.

# Whose needs are being met?

'Please appreciate me!' It's nice to be appreciated, isn't it? As brothers and sisters in Christ, we'll want to express appreciation to one another, and to encourage one another. But some people have a craving for appreciation which is totally out of control, and, although they don't actually walk around saying, 'Please appreciate me', they're obviously desperate for signs that others value them and think they're doing OK. The frequent doses of appreciation are needed to dull their inner pain. Just for a few minutes, or even for a few hours if they're lucky, someone else's kind words will silence the inner voices which tell them that they're no good and that nobody could possibly love them.

## *Compassion junkies*

Some individuals get their highs or dull their inner pain by helping lots of needy people. They've been called 'compassion junkies' because they are hooked on helping, and there are numerous parallels with other addictions. They are prepared to go to extraordinary lengths to help others. By this I don't mean that they do the decent Christian thing and put themselves out to help others, going the extra mile. I mean that they effectively destroy themselves in the process of helping others.

The logic goes something like this: if I rush around exhausting myself by caring for others and making sure that their pain is relieved and their neediness catered for, I'll see myself as a worthwhile member of the human race, and my inner emptiness won't hurt quite so much. Of course, it isn't usually said out loud quite like that, but the motivation is there, grumbling along not too far below the surface.

The motivation can become more obvious when the plan doesn't go quite as expected. Perhaps the person to be helped says 'No thanks' and rejects the offer. Or maybe they take the help time after time and don't have the decency to be grateful! Then the hidden volcano behind the 'compassion' erupts: 'After all I've done for them! Huh! I've worked myself to death to solve all their problems and spent money I couldn't afford to pay their bills, and they've just soaked it all up without a word of thanks. And now, to cap it all, they've complained that the holiday I arranged for them was a disaster because they hated being in the middle of nowhere surrounded by sheep!'

Now, if someone has been working themselves to death to solve someone else's problems, and paying their bills when they can't afford it, and arranging holidays which don't cater for the preferences of those who are going on them... the alarm bells start to ring. What's at work here isn't true compassion. The jargon word for it is *codependency*.

## Codependency

Codependency is another sort of counterfeit compassion. A person who is codependent is focused on the needs of others in a way that is closer to an addiction than to Christ-like *agape*-love. It's not really a cheap imitation, as the chapter title suggests. In fact, it can prove very costly—to the person doing the helping, to their family, and sometimes to the person being helped too.

Codependency was first recognized by those working with alcoholics. They noticed that it was not unusual for an alcoholic to have a particular friend or relative who continually bailed them out, figuratively if not literally. They rescued them from the police station or the gutter, washed away the vomit, telephoned the boss with a made-up excuse for their absence from work, and so on. They were called *enablers*, because their well-meaning intervention enabled the alcoholic to continue their addiction-driven lifestyle. In some cases whole families were effectively blocking recovery: their noble rallying round was preventing the alcoholic from feeling the full impact of his or her chosen behaviour. This took away much of the incentive for change.

*Codependents' lives are bent around other people's needs or behaviour*. Their helpful, caring exterior masks a 'black hole' of need and much personal pain. They find it virtually impossible to say 'No'. Troubled folk have a magnetic attraction for them—they are driven compulsively to attempt to sort out other people's lives. They also find it difficult to *hear* the word 'No', so may insist on 'helping' those who have no desire to be helped.

## Codependency is not love

Codependent caring is sometimes presented as *agape*-love. It is not! Codependent caring is a counterfeit form of love, which is driven by the needs of the person doing the caring and not by concern for others. *Agape*-love is *not* driven by need, does *not* depend upon a grateful response, and is able to be strong and say 'No' where necessary. *Agape*-love genuinely desires the *best* for the other person—not just their short-term happiness—and is willing to risk being thought of as uncaring if necessary.

Someone showing *agape*-love 'is not easily angered' (1 Corinthians 13:5), but could show anger under circumstances in which anger is an appropriate emotion. In contrast, a codependent person might seethe inside behind a slightly strained smile, or even a frown, but would attempt to mask any anger—until, that is, it became so uncontrollable that it burst out all over the place.

## Driven to help

Driven to help others, whatever the cost in terms of their own well-being, codependents give little thought to their own day-to-day needs. They grit their teeth, and keep the show on the road—whatever it takes. Their self-regard depends upon it. They may, for example, put time they can ill afford into sorting out another family's needs while their own family is falling apart. This sounds a crazy way to behave, but how many church leaders might, if pressed, have to admit to coming remarkably close to it?

The problem is that it doesn't work. Those they're helping very often don't respond in the way they had hoped. They find that the rainbows they've painted in other people's storms get washed away by the next deluge, often with nothing to show for all the effort they put in. Codependents gradually accumulate reservoirs of rage. People don't appreciate them as much as they should, and life's problems have an unhappy knack of failing to respond to their sure-fire remedies. How dare they!

Driven by their own unacknowledged needs, they feel there's no choice but to continue their thankless task. One day, everyone will be grateful for all their efforts. Or, at least, one day someone might notice how hard they're trying... Some church leaders struggle for years to fulfil everyone's impossible expectations, trying to meet everyone's needs and to help everyone who is hurting. When their health eventually breaks down, they see themselves as pitiful failures. But they're not failures—they're codependents! Codependents need to learn when to quit. They also need to learn to feel their own feelings.

## Feeling our own feelings

A codependent person will be able to tell us what others are feeling, sometimes with surprising accuracy. Codependents know what other people need, and are prepared to put lots of energy into seeing those needs met. But if we ask a codependent person what *they* are feeling, they may find it surprisingly difficult to give us a straight answer. Many codependents are so out of touch with their own feelings that they are incapable of giving a truthful response. They may look outside themselves in order to find an acceptable answer. For example, they may reason that because they are a Christian, and Christians are full of joy and peace, that they must be feeling joyful and peaceful. They may talk about their feelings in a very thinking-orientated way, for example saying 'I think it's sad' rather than 'I feel sad'. I know that I have to watch my tendency to *discuss* my feelings rather than *express* them.

Many Christians, not just those who are codependents, seem to think that feeling our own feelings is dangerous; they see it as the first step on a slippery slope towards being taken over by our feelings, and acting in ways we'll live to regret. This is not true—in fact, it's almost the opposite of the truth! If we squash our feelings, refusing to allow them to come to the surface, they may one day break out, taking us and everyone else by surprise. People who do things which others regard as totally out of character can be acting upon unacknowledged feelings which they have worked hard to suppress.

If we make it a habit to feel our feelings, and to own them—even the feelings which we think good Christians ought not to have—we are then in a position to choose, thoughtfully and prayerfully, how to respond to them. Acknowledging our feelings does not automatically put them in control; it simply makes them accessible, and less likely to pop up unexpectedly like a jack-in-the-box. Strong emotions need to be handled with particular care. If we're aware of their building up, we can choose an appropriate time and place to express them to God or to another person; if we pretend they don't exist they won't go away—they'll be ticking away like unexploded bombs which could go off at any time.

## Self-denial and cross-bearing

Christians who are locked into a treadmill of compulsive helping will sometimes justify it by saying that self-denial is scriptural. And self-denial *is* scriptural—but self-destruction isn't! Matthew, Mark and Luke all record Jesus' words: 'If anyone would come after me, he must deny himself and take up his cross daily and follow me' (Luke 9:23).

It is possible to read that verse with the emphasis in different places. Some will stress the importance of self-denial, and others will labour the daily carrying of the cross. Both are important, but I suspect that in order to do either the main focus needs to be on the last two words: 'follow me'. If we're following Jesus, rather than becoming self-absorbed in the process of self-denial (and becoming self-absorbed in the process of self-denial is easier than we might think)... if we're following Jesus, rather than focusing on the mighty big cross we're carrying... if we have our eyes on Jesus, we're less likely to get hooked into compulsive helping.

Following Jesus *can* get us into all sort of difficulties—Jesus went on to say: '...whoever loses his life for me will save it' (Luke 9:24). But when he said that, the emphasis was still on Jesus, on *following him*, not on deliberately destroying ourselves. Losing our life (physically or metaphorically) may be a by-product of our serving Jesus, but he never intends self-destruction to be our aim.

If we recognize that we've been preoccupied with self-denial or cross-bearing, or rushing from one needy person to another, we can ask God to restore our focus to where *he* wants it to be. We can ask God to shine his light of truth on our motives (and I do mean *our* motives—it's much easier to pray that God will shine his light on someone else's). We all have mixed motives—that's because we're all sinners. But rather than shrugging our shoulders and carrying on just the same, we could ask our compassionate, full-of-mercy God to help us to be more like Jesus—showing true compassion, not one of the counterfeits.

## True compassion in action

A legal expert's attempt at testing Jesus (Luke 10:25–29) prompted him to tell what has since become probably the best-known illustration of true compassion in action: the story of the good Samaritan.

### *Helper or helped?*

When seeking to apply this parable to church life, it can be tempting to try to decide who are the people lying half-dead beside the road, and who are the good Samaritans. Some may see me as a 'professional Samaritan'. Others who have come alongside in my difficult times will be aware that I do know what it is to be half-dead too! The truth is that at different times we can take both roles. Sometimes on our journey we can end up very battered and unable to continue. At other times we'll be God's person in the right place at the right time, to give a helping hand to a fellow traveller.

It's vital to extinguish the myth that those who help others are superhuman, because this leads to a second myth: that if I'm to help others I must pretend that I have no needs or struggles of my own. We must be as disciplined about making time for and accepting God's provision for our *own* needs as we are about making time for those of others, because otherwise we'll end up living a lie.

## *Wounded soldiers*

In the late 1980s, I and others at the church I then attended were greatly blessed by the Danny Daniels song 'I am a wounded soldier'.

> *I am a wounded soldier but I will not leave the fight*
> *because the Great Physician is healing me.*
> *So I'm standing in the battle, in the armour of His light,*
> *because His mighty power is real in me.*
> *I am loved, I am accepted by the Saviour of my soul.*
> *I am loved, I am accepted and my wounds will be made whole.*

The church was one in which many of us had received considerable healing, and in this song we were able both to acknowledge that, *and* to admit that we were still in the process of being made whole. In a way which is difficult to describe, this song was used by God to set me free from the burden of stereotyping (a doctor, accustomed to the role of helper), and to break down any barriers that might have appeared to exist between helper and helped. Together we were able to express vulnerability and our need for the touch of the Great Physician, and together we were able to share hope, love and acceptance.

As 'wounded soldiers' we were able help others, not by denying our woundedness and bustling on helping so that we didn't have time to feel our own pain, but by receiving fully from the Lord all that he had to give us, so that we had plenty to pass on to others. The apostle Paul was making the same point when he wrote: 'Praise be to the God and Father of our Lord Jesus Christ, the Father of compassion and the God of all comfort, who comforts us in all our troubles, so that we can comfort those in any trouble with the comfort we ourselves have received from God' (2 Corinthians 1:3–4). It's much easier to go on passing on that which we're going on receiving! (The subjects of healthy interdependence, and compassion without codependency, are further explored in Study 7 at the end of the book.)

## Not abandoning our journey

Have you ever noticed that, after giving the injured man the urgent help he needed, the good Samaritan carried on with his own journey, promising to call in on his way back? The Samaritan didn't abandon his journey in order to found a hospital for wounded travellers!

God doesn't usually ask us to stop travelling altogether, abandoning *our* journey in order to centre our life upon a wounded person we've found beside the road. It may be necessary for a while to suspend normal activities and put our own needs and plans on hold, in order to give our full attention to a crisis or a longer-term situation that demands our attention. But we need to check from time to time that we're in the right place. Is this particular caring role part of God's plan for us, or have we allowed a need to be the one who sorts things out to keep us involved in a situation for longer than the Lord intended?

## Keeping our focus on God

The only person who has the right to take the central place in our lives is God. If he is at the centre, then his *agape*-love and his compassion will flow through us; if we make needy folk the centre of our lives, we're sliding into idolatry. If we've allowed any*thing* or any*one* to take God's rightful place, we need to ask him for forgiveness and healing, and his help in moving on to be the people he intends us to be. Then we'll be better equipped to respond to the challenge of showing his *agape*-love and his compassion to a needy world.

If the focus which should have been on God has been hijacked by feelings of being worthless, unloved and unlovable, we need to take such feelings to him, *in order to dethrone them*. If our feelings are very painful, the idea of facing them and bringing them to God may sound really scary, and finding an anaesthetic, such as helping others and focusing on their problems, may sound preferable. But this does not honour God, and it will not meet our needs either. As we bring our feelings to God, we need to allow the teaching of the Bible to shape our thinking about ourselves; this will in turn affect our feelings and contribute to the healing process.

However we show compassion, it can be quite draining, and we may often feel that we're simply not up to it. We need to go on asking God to make us more aware of *his* love and compassion. If we can really lay hold of what he's like, and draw close enough to sense his love, his mercy, his compassion, perhaps we won't need to wear ourselves to a frazzle trying to earn approval, being driven beyond his call by nagging doubts about our worth. We need to allow the Father of compassion and the God of all comfort to draw alongside us, and to teach us to pace ourselves according to the rhythms of his grace. By keeping the focus on him, we'll be better able to show his compassion to others.

## Compassion for one another

When looking at the subject of compassion, our thoughts go to the desperately needy people out there in a needy world, and those we know nearer to home in heart-rending situations. That's right and proper, because we do need to share God's heart with those in need. But there is an additional dimension to compassion.

Paul writes: 'Be kind and compassionate to one another, forgiving each other, just as in Christ God forgave you.' (Ephesians 4:32) The word 'compassionate' here isn't the bowel-churning, heart-rending word we've been focusing on. It's a different Greek word, which in some versions is translated 'tender-hearted'. I'm sure there's a reason for using this different word. Paul is urging the Ephesians to be kind and compassionate to *one another*—to those they met with regularly, the ordinary folk around them. He's not talking about particularly needy people, or those with heart-rending stories of suffering. He's talking about the very men and women whose ordinariness or apparent lack of problems—or the fact that we see them at the front of the church doing things, or in leadership roles or behind the tea urn every week so they *must* be OK—may mean that we don't feel moved to compassion when we see them. It's about our attitude to these people that Paul is writing.

It comes in the context (Ephesians 4:26–27) of a warning about the dangers of allowing anger to provide the evil one with a foothold. Paul is telling the Ephesians to acknowledge and deal with their anger rather than letting it fester. In the following chapter they're encouraged to live as children of light, to find out what pleases the Lord, and to have nothing to do with what Paul calls 'the fruitless deeds of darkness' (Ephesians 5:11).

In the midst of all this, Paul writes: 'Be kind and compassionate to one another, forgiving each other, just as in Christ God forgave you' (Ephesians 4:32). The word 'forgiving' in this verse could also be translated 'gracing'—'gracing one another'. This verse speaks to me of the generosity of spirit which we all need as we seek to serve the Lord together.

Just as our compassion for the needy people around us, and those in the trouble spots of the world, needs to be genuine, so also we need to show true compassion and kindness to those around us and to the members of our families—whether or not they are obviously in need. Codependent caring will focus on helping those with glaring needs as being the more certain route to a feeling of having done something worthwhile. *Agape*-love loves without any thought of return, or 'brownie points' earned, and just loves.

When asked to write a review of pastoral care in the church I attend, I entitled it 'Pastoral care is for everyone!' This served to underline that pastoral care is not just for a few people who are somehow inadequate or especially needy—any more than it is for a select few to give to others! We all blossom when we experience the love of God being shared with us by those walking along with us in the Christian life. Pastoral care and compassion aren't just for 'wimps'; we all need them, so we need to repent of any pride that prevents us being on the receiving end.

## Compassion for codependents too

It's easy to become irritated with those we see trying to meet their own needs through compulsively helping others. If only they'd realize how silly it is, and take care of themselves and their families, then we wouldn't have to pour so many pastoral resources into bailing them out when it all gets too much! But codependents can believe at a very deep level that their very survival depends on their taking care of the needs of others.

This may be because as a child they had to tiptoe round, ready to respond to every whim of a drunken or controlling parent, in order to avoid their wrath. They learned that the way to meet their own need for safety was to give full attention to someone else's needs. The same danger may no longer be there (although it may be—for example, many children of alcoholics marry spouses who turn out to be alcoholics) but they continue to protect themselves in the same way; it has become a habit. They don't feel free to choose to do differently, so it's no good just lecturing them.

For similar reasons, people can find it very difficult to reveal their own neediness, preferring the spotlight to be on the neediness of others. This may be because for them it has never been safe to be needy. Perhaps they've felt they had to maintain an air of invincibility because an abusive parent punished them every time they cried, shouting '*I'll* give you something to cry about'.

## *Healthy patterns of caring*

We all need to develop a sense of our own worth which is independent from our caring or other roles. We need a sense of worth which allows us to be vulnerable and to admit to having needs, without feeling devalued. We need to find genuine security, and healing for our wounds. And we all need to have healthy patterns of caring behaviour modelled to us, consistently. This is quite a challenge—one that today's church cannot afford to sidestep.

How healthy are our patterns of caring? Are they rooted in and empowered by *agape*-love—or are they driven by unacknowledged neediness on the part of the carers? If church members are running themselves into the ground looking after all and sundry, while neglecting their own families, are they likely to be challenged? Are folk blossoming as a result of pastoral care which encourages them in their growth as people and as disciples, or is the emphasis on keeping them happy, or telling them what they ought to be doing and keeping them under control?

True compassion reflects God's nature, and underlines that we are our Father's children. Let's not become preoccupied with doing things which we hope will make us feel better about ourselves, or settle for people-pleasing or one of the other counterfeits, when we could be knowing and sharing the real thing.

# Focus point

'Do I bustle on, trying to forget my own needs and wounds? Or do I make a habit of receiving from God so that I have plenty to pass on?'

Read 2 Corinthians 1:3–4. Do you know God as 'the Father of compassion and the God of all comfort'?

'Am I happy to receive help from others, or am I only comfortable in the role of helper?'

For some people, choosing to accept God's grace can be the first step towards learning to accept help from others. Ask your heavenly Father to help you if you find this difficult.

Ask those closest to you: 'What is the cost to you of the help I give to those in need?'

Listen carefully and patiently to their answers, and reflect on your feelings about them. Take your thoughts and feelings to God. Ask him to shine his light into your situation.

# Religion or relationship?

### John 8:31–32

*Jesus said, 'If you hold to my teaching, you are really my disciples.*
*Then you will know the truth, and the truth will set you free.'*

*This is my happiness:*
*God is my Father and I am His child.*

Mother Basilea Schlink

The English word 'religion' comes from the Latin *religio*. This is thought to have its root in the Latin verb *ligio* which means 'I bind'. It's from this Latin verb that we get our word 'ligature'. I remember someone explaining this to me when I was a teenager, and since then I've been uncomfortable about Christianity being described as a religion—after all, it's supposed to be about being set free, not about coming into bondage.

Of course, there are aspects of our faith which it's reasonable to describe as religious in the generally accepted meaning of that word, but it's vital that they're not pursued in the absence of a relationship with God. Religion without relationship is a real bind!

So, the truth sets free, but the church... What does the church do? I meet many Christians who are permanently tired. Their diaries are full. They're running on empty. They'd like to stop the treadmill and get off, but they don't have a spare minute in which to think how they might go about it. They feel *bound* to continue.

# What does God look for?

I believe that a misunderstanding of what God requires of his people can contribute to this undesirable state of affairs. For example, it's possible to read the verse at the beginning of this chapter in more than one way. It could be taken to mean that, if we know all the facts there are to know about Jesus, and study the Bible devotedly, we'll find a freedom that comes from such a wealth of knowledge. This isn't what Jesus meant.

## *Discipleship versus religious knowledge*

The Greek word translated 'know' is the verb *ginosko*, which is used to speak of knowing a person rather than knowing facts. Vine's *Complete Expository Dictionary of Old and New Testament Words* says: 'In the New Testament *ginosko* frequently indicates a relation between the person "knowing" and the object known... The verb is also used to convey the thought of connection or union, as between man and woman.' The knowing that sets free comes from the language of intimacy not the language of scholarship.

Knowing what we believe is important, but Jesus' disciples were called 'disciples' because they travelled day by day along the same road as he did, and sought to follow his teaching. They didn't just memorize it and store it away. True disciples are those who desire to know Christ intimately, and to become like him. As the saying goes: 'It's not *what* you know, it's *who* you know'! It's about developing and being changed by a relationship, rather than becoming an expert super-Christian who knows all the answers, keeps all the rules and does all the right things.

Jesus spoke of himself as 'the truth'. By that he meant more than 'the answer to difficult questions'. The idea of knowing the answer to everything is a seductive one, especially for those who feel insecure or insignificant. But remember how Jesus spoke about the religious experts of his day.

## *Following Jesus versus religious activity*

An outsider looking into the church might be forgiven for believing that the most important acquisition for someone who becomes a Christian is a new diary! There are meetings to be made a priority, schedules of devotions to be followed, and so much to be learned. Is it possible that a new convert who sets out to know Jesus better might be sidetracked rather than helped by the wealth of activities?

Going to church, listening to teaching, studying the Bible at home, attending discipleship classes and prayer meetings... These may help us to get to know Jesus intimately. But they can also be steps in a religious process, and be pursued compulsively without any sense of intimacy at all.

'Religious processes' may sound empty and boring, but what they lack in excitement they more than make up for in security. They are predictable and measurable. We have some idea what we're letting ourselves in for. Time spent reading the Bible and praying can be controlled, whereas a relationship... that sounds unpredictable, perhaps even risky. We need to remember that God is neither safe nor predictable; anything which tries to make him so is leading us away from him, even if in the short term it makes us feel more secure.

A living, growing faith *will* lead to actions, some of which might be described as religious activities, but they're meant to be the out-working of faith, not its mainstay. We need to be willing to check that we're not unintentionally sending new Christians down the road of religion to the exclusion of relationship.

And what about those who have been Christians for many years? The Bible tells us that as Christians we must expect to endure trials and tribulations, but how many Christians in leadership, if asked to draw up a list of the main trials in their lives, would include church meetings? Many feel trapped inside a treadmill which brings round the next meeting before they've had time to process the paperwork from the last one. If that's how we feel, how can we plan our escape?

## Redefining our priorities

If we attended only those meetings which contributed towards our knowing God more intimately and following him more effectively (and following him inevitably includes considering the well-being of others, so the statement is not as individualistic as it may sound), what would be the result? If the long meetings many of us attend were pruned so that time was spent only on matters which contributed to our knowing God more intimately and following him more effectively, would we end up getting the sleep we may currently be missing?

Probably. But then so many important things would never be discussed, such as which design of cups should be purchased for the church hall (and *should* new cups be purchased at all while people are starving in the developing world?) Should the exterior woodwork of the pastor's house be re-painted this year or left until next? Should the youth group be asked to pay for the light-bulbs they broke while playing over-exuberant volleyball in the hall? We can no doubt think of many other examples.

Of course responsible decision-making is vital in any church. Many decisions need to be taken, and taken carefully. What we should question is whether they're being taken in the most effective way. Maybe those aspects of church which feel 'a bind' are soaking up too much time and energy, leaving little to put into building our relationship with Jesus and encouraging others to know and follow him. Some things do need to be sorted out at meetings, but many don't. In some matters (such as the pattern on the church hall cups), all that is required is to choose one of several alternatives. If the level of trust within a fellowship is such that even this sort of decision can't agreeably be delegated, there's something seriously wrong.

Other matters are more complex, yet still don't need the accumulated wisdom of an entire committee; they can safely be entrusted to one or two individuals whose spiritual gift (for example, the gift of administration) has equipped them for the task. This approach not only prevents time being taken away from priority issues—it can lead to the job being done more effectively too. I'm reminded of the old joke about the camel being a horse that was designed by a committee!

We may laugh at the Pharisees—their preoccupation with correctness in things which we can see quite clearly didn't matter, like tithing garden herbs (Matthew 23:23). We can see so clearly that they really ought to have been concentrating on the things which were on God's heart, like justice, mercy and faithfulness. But is it possible that our preoccupations and enthusiasms might look equally bizarre to someone else? Have we ever paused to consider how God views them?

# Developing the relationship

Are we prepared to take the risk of making intimacy with God a priority? And I do mean an enduring priority, not just something we focus on for a day or two in order to straighten ourselves out, before moving on.

## *Knowing God's heart*

When did you last ask God what was on *his* heart? And waited for an answer? Does taking time out for unhurried and unstructured communion with the Lord sound like a luxury? If today we were to open our diaries and ask Jesus how he saw them, what would he say? Would his priorities for our time be those which our diaries reflect?

A relationship does not flourish if there is little contact. It would seem unnecessary to say this, but my experience is that although people usually agree that it's true, they often act as if it were not! The title of a book by Bill Hybels, the Willow Creek pastor—*Too Busy Not To Pray*—hit the nail on the head. But how many Christian workers are attempting to engage in major ministries while their relationship with their heavenly Father is distant? The first casualty of growing demands upon their time was their daily devotions.

Jesus said to his disciples during their final briefing in the upper room: 'I am the way and the truth and the life. No one comes to the Father except through me' (John 14:6). Jesus is saying that a relationship with him is not just *a* way to the Father, but the *only* way. What are late-night meetings discussing church hall cups and exterior paintwork (perhaps our modern equivalent of tithing garden herbs) doing to our relationship with Jesus? Not to mention what they're doing to our relationship with the husband or wife we promised to love and to cherish.

## But what sort of relationship?

We'll also need to ask ourselves from time to time what *sort* of relationship we're developing with God. In Revelation we can read what God had to say to the church in Ephesus. He had observed their gritted teeth, well exercised discernment, and determination not to quit, but something was lacking: 'I know your deeds, your hard work and your perseverance. I know that you cannot tolerate wicked men, that you have tested those who claim to be apostles but are not, and have found them to be false. You have persevered and have endured hardships for my name, and have not grown weary. Yet I hold this against you: You have forsaken your first love' (Revelation 2:2–4).

They were doing so much that was right! Yet the passage seems to be saying that fiercely dutiful but loveless obedience is not enough.

## Commanding Officer

I was reminded of this when my son, David, preached at our church on a weekend home. He shared how he had come to realize that he saw God as a commanding officer who required his obedience. Yes, he did know about God's love, but he didn't particularly feel the need to experience it. He saw it as a luxury—not really necessary for a good soldier. All God had to do was bark out the orders and he'd do as he was told. The love aspect was all very well but he could cope without it.

God showed David a picture of himself: he was in a huge banqueting hall, and God was showing him to his seat. 'Here it is,' God said, pointing to a seat at the main table. David looked around at all the finery and at the proffered seat. 'This isn't for me,' he said. 'I don't belong here.' He turned to make his way back to his place in the slaves' quarters. Over a period of a few weeks God graciously showed David in a variety of ways that he wanted to relate to him as a loving father, not as a commanding officer—that love was *not* an optional refinement to the relationship. *God is love!* (1 John 4:8). Without love there is no relationship. Without love, Christian service is noisy emptiness (1 Corinthians 13:1–3).

Anne Long, in her book *Listening*, tells of how the god of her childhood liked lots of noise, especially loud music from Salvation Army bands, and had a long beard. Her god had a lot in common with William Booth, who founded the Salvation Army, and whose photograph hung in her grandparents' home. She writes: 'I remember puzzling over how busy he always seemed to be, especially on Sundays when, if you wanted to stay in his good books, you went to as many meetings as possible. If I'd been less frightened of him I'd have asked him why he didn't approve of family time and fun together on Sundays. But I never dared.'

Canon Long says that she was frightened of her childhood god. Even as an adult, having come to faith, she used to feel panicky about going to church. She goes on: 'I can still sometimes catch myself out as I approach prayer with negative expectations of doom and gloom... As the old image withers in the light of his reality and the distortions gradually give way to his truth, I am finding he really is the God of surprises and I am drawn to him' (Anne Long, *Listening*).

## Like Father, like son or daughter

In the introduction to this book I posed the question: what does my life say about what I believe about God and what he requires of me? Whether or not we're consciously aware of our answer, it's these beliefs which fashion our relationship with God. If we've spent years believing that he's a nit-picking perfectionist, a tyrannical slave-driver, or a capricious prima donna, our relationship with him will have developed accordingly. These beliefs about God may also have had an effect on the way we've developed as a person. Someone who daily attempts the impossible, trying to please a disagreeable boss or parent, tends to develop attitudes which affect the way they see themselves—and resentments which can affect their other relationships too.

Jesus emphasized his Father-likeness, even going to the extent of saying: 'Do not believe me unless I do what my Father does' (John 10:37). He had already criticized the Jews, who prided themselves on being children of Abraham, pointing out that the way they behaved showed that they were children of the devil

(John 8:39–44). If someone came to your church and assumed 'Like Father, like son', what deductions would they make about God's character? Has your individual character been allowed to develop fully within a healthy relationship with God, or been squashed by trying to relate to one of the caricatures?

## *Are we able to tell God how we feel?*

Elijah is remembered as a spiritual giant who accomplished great things for God, but he had his less triumphant moments too. I was speaking about workaholism to a group of church leaders and Christian doctors who meet occasionally to look at topics of mutual interest. Towards the end of what I had to say, I displayed the following words on the overhead projector: 'Elijah... went a day's journey into the desert. He came to a broom tree, sat down under it and prayed that he might die. "I have had enough, Lord..."' (1 Kings 19:4).

It was clear from the response that many of those present were able to identify with Elijah. But how many would have dared to give a hint of their feelings in any other gathering? And how many felt able to express these feelings to God? Was their relationship with him such that they would risk it?

Elijah had boldly confronted the prophets of Baal on Mount Carmel (1 Kings 18:21–40), and God had shown his power in a very dramatic way. This had upset Jezebel so much that she had sent Elijah a death-threat. He ran for his life. He sent his servant away, and went alone into the desert. There, Elijah did the unthinkable. He said to God: 'I quit.' What was God's response? Did he lecture Elijah on his lack of faith or perseverance? Did he obliterate him with a thunderbolt, saying 'Let that be a lesson to all who dare to be less than enthusiastic in my service'? Did he withdraw from Elijah and leave him to die in the desert? Not at all. He allowed Elijah to catch up on some much-needed sleep, and then delivered breakfast.

After some more rest, and another dose of nourishment, God sent Elijah on a long and apparently solitary walk, after which he was able to rest in a cave. Only then did God ask, very gently, that Elijah explain himself. The Lord then proceeded to reveal something of his true nature to Elijah. He also corrected Elijah's perceptions which had become rather distorted during his stressful time. No, he wasn't really the only follower of God left; it only *felt* like it.

Put yourself in Elijah's place and ask: if I were to say that sort of thing to God, how would I expect him to respond? It is unlikely that God's response to you would be identical, but it would still be true to his nature, which doesn't change. I suspect that many people under pressure fear that telling God how they really feel, or even saying 'I quit', is guaranteed to make matters worse. This is partly due to the fact that, when we are stressed, our assessment of the situation can be as inaccurate as Elijah's was. However, a major influence comes from our accumulated beliefs about God and the resulting picture of him which we carry with us. This can distort our relationship with him, such that we are relating to a caricature of God rather than to God himself.

Elijah's saying 'I quit' was the starting point in a process of restoration. This began with *physical refreshment*. So often when we or others are burned out we feel the need to do something religious. That's not how God dealt with Elijah. I don't believe that God is nearly as religious as we make him out to be! From time to time I suggest to weary or frustrated Christians that they go down to the beach and throw stones in the sea. This apparently pointless activity, which comes with no instructions about how many stones to throw or how often to do it, is a simple way of learning to take time for no purpose other than refreshment—something driven people find very difficult. Some can only cope with throwing stones into the sea if they're allowed to turn it into a skimming contest, striving to find stones of the shape most likely to achieve an even greater number of hops.

'Get away with me and you'll recover your life,' says Jesus. 'I'll show you how to take a real rest' (Matthew 11:28, *The Message*). What, I wonder, did Jesus have in mind when he said this? Might it have included a walk by the Sea of Galilee? Jesus went on (v. 30) to say 'Keep company with me…' Perhaps that's a good place to start, but let's not assume that keeping company with Jesus will automatically mean doing religious things.

# Abiding

Jesus really knew the Father. He had been 'keeping company' with him since the foundation of the world. He didn't have to wonder what the Father was like: he knew. And he reflected the Father's true nature in his life. Jesus did only what he saw the Father doing (John 5:19), and spoke only what the Father commanded him to say (John 12:49). He was rejected by the religious experts but, as he faced his imminent death, he looked on going to the Father as *going home*. He was going to be with the Father who had been dwelling in him all through his ministry, the Father who had been walking in a moment-by-moment relationship with him.

## At home with the Lord

But what about us? We might be tempted to think that it was OK for Jesus, and perhaps OK for the disciples. But the scriptures challenge us to look for a moment-by-moment relationship too. In John 14:17 Jesus talks about the Holy Spirit living, abiding, dwelling within. He goes on (John 14:23): 'If anyone loves me, he will obey my teaching. My Father will love him, and we will come to him and *make our home with* him.'

John, writing in his first letter, puts our position very clearly: 'If anyone acknowledges that Jesus is the Son of God, God *lives in* him and he in God' (1 John 4:15). John uses the same word used by Jesus when he said 'make our home with him', which can also be translated dwelling, abiding, or remaining.

Just as in Jesus' day, some people today feel that to talk about a personal relationship with God is offensive, a manifestation of spiritual pride. But the biblical view is that we *are* intended to have a really close relationship. Jesus says: 'On that day you will realize that I am in my Father, and you are in me, and I am in you' (John 14:20). That sounds pretty personal! But in one sense it's up to us. Will 'going to the Father' feel like going home? Or shall we go to be with a Father we hardly know, because we've spent our lives trying to serve a caricature?

## *A neglected relationship?*

Jesus cautioned his disciples about the perils of losing touch—of neglecting the very relationship which was to be the source of their strength and fruitfulness: 'Remain in me, and I will remain in you. No branch can bear fruit by itself; it must remain in the vine. Neither can you bear fruit unless you remain in me. I am the vine; you are the branches. If a man remains in me and I in him, he will bear much fruit; apart from me you can do nothing' (John 15:4–5).

Clive Calver, while he was still head of the Evangelical Alliance, wrote:

> *It is easy for us to love Christ's work; to love the ministry opportunities we have through our churches; to love the way he uses and blesses us. And yet how vital it is to remind ourselves—especially at a time of relative 'success'—that ultimately it is not what we do but who we are in God that counts... I keep having to remind myself of what must come first... 'Not my activity for God, but my intimacy with him.'*

> (*IDEA* magazine, April–May 1997)

Have we become so list-driven, so caught up in the cycle of church meetings, counselling, pastoring and so on that we've neglected any sort of relationship... being so busy 'doing for God', perhaps even making sacrifices for him, that we've not had a moment to sit with him and hear what's on *his* heart? Have those close to us heard us talking freely and enthusiastically about our faith, and seen our love of the Lord in our faces? Or do they only ever hear us talk (and see us frown?) about 'church'?

## *On active service*

Christians are called to serve; service is not an optional extra for the extra-keen ones—it's an integral part of discipleship. Jesus made it clear that the serving is to flow out of an abiding relationship with God, but so often 'serving' and 'abiding' seem to end up in opposition to one another; it's a case of one or the other but not both!

As a result of our restored relationship with God, life and eternity are held secure; this should be immensely freeing, and service should be a joyful part of the result. But those who serve in order to find the significance they feel they lack, or to earn God's favour, will serve with a determination brought about by fear and uncertainty. Our heavenly Father longs for us to serve him without fear, and drawn by love, rather than by a compulsion stemming from our unhealed wounds.

I need to be willing to ask myself from time to time whether the Lord's service feels like the 'perfect freedom' he intends it to be, or whether I've slipped into a spiritual-looking form of bondage, a 'hardening of the oughteries'. I need to ask whether my serving is flowing out of my relationship with God, or getting in the way of it. The sad thing about putting lots of energy into trying to keep everything going, doing church, showing God how hard we're trying, gritting our teeth and refusing to quit, is that it sidetracks us from the intimacy which our heavenly Father wants us to have with him, and from the peace he longs to bring to our lives. For further thoughts on intimacy with God, and on the subject of peace, see Study 8 at the end of the book.

The temptation can be to add 'intimacy with God' to the long list of things we need to do! Bishop Graham Dow writes:

> *We live in a very busy and stressful culture. We have to run to stand still. There is pressure of work and pressure of family life; it all has us constantly thinking, 'What must I do next?' ... But, so easily we can hide behind all this busyness and never meet God. It is often only when God strips away all that 'we must do next', that we have the space to have profound dealings with him.*

> Pathways of Prayer, edited by Graham Dow

Are we willing to come out of denial—to accept that frantic effort and ceaseless activity can side-track us from what God really does require of us?

## *So what does God require?*

First of all, he requires us to face the truth about ourselves, and to choose his way of dealing with what we're really like—receiving cleansing and forgiveness through the blood of Jesus. Asking God for forgiveness necessitates coming out from behind any façade we may have built, abandoning our fortress of self-sufficiency—perhaps even dropping the drawbridge we've pulled up between our leadership and everyone else's followership—and joining the rest of the human race. Each one of us comes before God to face the same harsh reality: 'If we claim to be without sin, we deceive ourselves... and make [God] out to be a liar...' (1 John 1:8 and 10).

What else does God require of us? The prophet Micah asks: 'And what does the Lord require of you?' and goes on to answer: 'To act justly and to love mercy and to walk humbly with your God' (Micah 6:8). I've already written about how a friend came to understand the importance of acting justly *as well as* loving mercy (see page 73). But what about the third part: walking humbly with God. What does this mean in practice?

# Walking humbly with God

I have read that Agnes Sandford, the writer and teacher on inner healing, shared at a conference how one day she was about to get on a plane, and felt that God was telling her not to. She didn't get on it, and it crashed. By taking notice of what God was saying to her—by walking humbly with God rather than saying 'You cannot be serious'—her life was saved.

## *'Are you sure, God?'*

I have had less dramatic examples of the value of acting on a prompting from God. For example, I'd been thinking for three or four months that it would be useful to have a flip-chart stand to use in the counselling teaching I do. It really hadn't seemed that urgent, and I hadn't done anything about it, but one morning during my quiet time I felt that the Lord was saying to me that it was the day to go and buy a flip-chart stand.

I phoned up the local supplier of that sort of equipment who told me about the various options they had in stock or to order. I said I'd call in later that day. When I arrived, the first person I saw was the friendly chap who works in the second-hand section. He greeted me cheerfully and asked me what I was looking for. I explained that I had come to buy a flip-chart stand. 'Well,' he said, 'you've chosen the right day to come!' Only hours earlier, they had taken delivery of some second-hand but unused flip-chart stands, which they would be selling at a fraction of their new price!

I remember being really excited—not just because it saved me a lot of money, but mainly because I felt that God was using it to underline to me that he's with me in the teaching I do. I shared it with a few people, some of whom were delighted and thanked God, and others... well, they gave me slightly odd looks. The trouble is, once we start sharing this sort of thing, some may start saying (or, for politeness' sake, thinking, but not saying), 'Oh it's all right for her, she's got a personal hotline to God'!

When Agnes Sandford shared at the conference about not getting on the plane, a lady button-holed her afterwards and went on about how unfair it was that God had spoken only to Agnes Sandford, and had allowed all the others on the plane to go to their death. 'Oh,' said Agnes, 'I'm *sure* he was speaking to all the others as well!'

## Humble enough to listen

Whatever people may think or feel, it's not a matter of a few privileged individuals having personal hotlines to God! The lines are there for everyone, and God speaks to everyone, but not everyone 'picks up the phone' and listens. Walking humbly with God will include being humble enough—yes, humble enough—to listen to God, and being willing to act upon what he says. Of course, we have to be willing to look daft when we hear wrong. I've followed what I thought was a prompting from God and ended up in a blind alley quite a few times over the years! But we have to be willing to risk looking foolish—it's the only way to learn.

We need to practise discerning God's voice amidst all the other voices around us. Sometimes our own emotions can shout quite loudly and we can think it's God speaking. (Remember Recluse Ministries!) Obviously if we think he's saying something dramatic like 'Give up your job immediately' or 'Give all the church's money to the first person you see when you walk out of the door', we'll be wise to share it with someone whose spiritual judgment we trust, and to pray it through, to make sure that we haven't got our wires crossed.

But if we practise hearing him in not particularly dangerous situations—for example, heeding his inner prompting to phone someone who is in the middle of a crisis we didn't know about— if we walk humbly with him under these sorts of circumstances, then our ears will be tuned in, ready for when he needs to tell us to get off a plane or something equally serious. *And*, even more importantly, we'll be developing our relationship with the Lord.

## Spiritual disciplines

Part of walking humbly with God is acknowledging that we have much to learn and much growing to do. The saints of old practised a variety of 'spiritual disciplines', including prayer, fasting, solitude and reading the Bible, and these can, if rightly used, contribute towards our spiritual growth. But these days some Christians seem reluctant to embrace even the *idea* of spiritual discipline. Well aware that such practices can become an end in themselves rather than a route by which to travel, they reason that it's better to steer clear of them altogether. This would seem to me to have all the hallmarks of a strategy of the enemy: lead some Christians to overemphasize something, or to use it in an unhealthy way, so that other Christians react by rejecting it.

Both Old and New Testament writers condemned spiritual discipline-type practices, but only in so far as they had seen them being abused. Spiritual disciples are processes, tools if you like, which can be used to good effect or bad. Firemen don't abandon the hatchets they use to free those trapped in burning buildings just because they hear reports that hatchets have been used to kill people; they know that a hatchet is only a tool, which can be used for a variety of purposes according to the intent of the hand in which it is grasped.

Baptist minister and philosopher Dallas Willard emphasizes the value of the disciplines as part of a deliberate plan for spiritual growth and preparation for the trials which will come our way. No champion athlete would just turn up for an event and rely on getting by; he would take time to prepare beforehand. Willard writes:

> It is part of the misguided and whimsical condition of
> humankind that we so devoutly believe in the power of effort-at-
> the-moment-of-action alone to accomplish what we want and

*completely ignore the need for character change in our lives as a whole. The general human failing is to want what is right and important, but at the same time not to commit ourselves to the kind of life that will produce the action we know to be right and the condition we want to enjoy. This is the feature of human character that explains why the road to hell is paved with good intentions. We intend what is right, but we avoid the life that would make it a reality.*

Dallas Willard, *The Spirit of the Disciplines*

We probably all know teenagers who, having told us enthusiastically of their dreams of higher education or a career, have had to accept less appealing options because they only dreamed dreams and never got down to the hard work. It's easy to mutter about adolescent immaturity and the need to grow up and behave responsibly, but if we were to subject our own desire for closeness with God to the same scrutiny, would we have to admit that the good intentions and the dreams outnumbered the disciplined choices? Are we really walking humbly with God, or are we behaving like spiritual adolescents, sure that we already know everything that's worth knowing?

## Choosing to 'look up and out'

Mario Bergner is now an ordained minister at the Church of the Resurrection, Wheaton, Chicago. He is happily married with two children, and is the director of *Redeemed Life*, a ministry of pastoral care for the sexually broken. He was an actor and voice teacher when he felt challenged by God to seek healing and give up his homosexual lifestyle. He has written about the things he found helpful when he chose to reorientate his life. Having read Brother Lawrence's book *The Practice of the Presence of God*, he resolved to try to call on the name of Jesus with increasing frequency. This was designed to help him to learn to 'look up and out' of his problems and temptations, rather than allowing them to be the focal point of his life. It was as difficult as it sounds, but he persevered, taking care not to condemn himself when he forgot. 'After a while, I found if I forgot to practise God's presence, I would be reminded by the Spirit within me to do so… Soon I noticed that whenever my thoughts would wander, they would wander towards Him' (Mario Bergner, *Setting Love in Order: Hope and Healing for the Homosexual*).

Our minds are such that they *will* stray from time to time. If we are anxious about a particular difficulty, our thoughts will stray often in that direction. Continually rehearsing our anxieties, turning them over and over in our minds, can act as a fertilizer—helping them to grow! We need to practise the discipline which turns our anxieties into prayers and then refocuses. Similarly, repeated contemplation of a besetting sin weakens our resistance to temptation. How much better, therefore, to train our minds so that when they wander—as they inevitably will—they wander towards Jesus himself, towards the light rather than darkness.

Loving God with all our heart, soul, strength and mind is about being willing to walk day by day with God, allowing our daily walk to bear the hallmark of his indwelling presence, of his *shalom*, which means peace in the fullest sense. (See Study 8 for a more detailed explanation of the meaning of this Hebrew word.) It's about a relationship, rather than a set of rules and rituals or a diary full of meetings. It's about letting God deal with the unpalatable realities of our lives, and being changed on the inside. It's about choosing to obey God rather than men. We can't discipline ourselves into a relationship with God. But once, by grace, we have entered such a relationship, spiritual disciplines can help us to keep our focus on him, and to avoid those things which would distance us from him.

## *What—or who— is of central importance?*

Several years ago, I was aware of God speaking to me through a song which I learned with the church choir. It had a haunting refrain about the Lord being the centre of my life. I found myself singing it a lot, and being challenged as I did so: '*Who* is the centre of your life? *Who*?' I wrestled with the question over many months. It was one I couldn't just answer and move on; it needs answering for the rest of my days. '*Who* is the centre of my life?'

As a result of this challenge, I haven't ceased to be 'me', with my off-beat sense of humour, my liking for curries and certain types of chocolate, my love of reading, my likes and dislikes when it comes to clothes and music. I am still 'me'—that's the only person I'm qualified to be. And I haven't been miraculously translated to some higher plane of spirituality within which there are no temptations, no aggravations, no weariness, no meetings to attend and no difficult decisions to be made.

The main difference is perhaps that in any given situation I'm primarily interested in what God is saying. I'm aware that I need that close relationship with him so that I can do what I see him doing, working where I see him at work (and not labouring fruitlessly where he is not at work) and seeking to speak what he gives me to say. 'I press on to take hold of that for which Christ Jesus took hold of me' (Philippians 3:12).

# Focus point

**'Deep in my heart, the picture I have of God is of a...'**

- Commanding officer?

- Vague elderly grandfather?

- Perfectionistic quality control supervisor?

- Frowning school teacher?

- Impersonal official, only interested in rules?

What's *your* picture? Take time to reflect.

Bring your picture to your heavenly Father, and tell him about it, whether or not you feel it's a correct picture. (If it's what's in your heart, he already knows about it anyway.) If your picture is a distorted one, ask him where it's coming from. You could ask a friend to pray with you about this.

**'When I come to the end of my days, what will be my regrets?'**

Will you regret spending so much time on church business?... at work?... doing what?

Will you wish you'd spent more time on... what?

# 9

# Where do we go from here?

## Matthew 11:28–30 (*The Message*)

*'Are you tired? Worn out? Burned out on religion? Come to me.*
*Get away with me and you'll recover your life. I'll show you how*
*to take a real rest. Walk with me and work with me—watch how*
*I do it. Learn the unforced rhythms of grace. I won't lay anything*
*heavy or ill-fitting on you. Keep company with me and you'll*
*learn to live freely and lightly.'*

In the course of this book we've looked at the roots of drivenness and how it can blight our lives and the lives of those around us. We've seen that some things done in God's name are not only outside his plan but are directly contrary to his purposes. As we've looked at the way Jesus handled people and situations, maybe we've sensed that things *should* and *could* be different, and been attracted to the 'rhythms of grace' he talked about. So where do we start?

As with any personal journey, each of us starts from a different place. There's no mass prescription. There's no magic answer. But there are a few steps which are worth considering honestly, to see if they might apply to us, either as part of a recovery process or as part of a journey of discipleship and personal growth.

The first step, without which it's difficult to make progress on any of the others, is to come out of denial—to stop pretending there isn't really a problem—well, not one that needs taking seriously, not *that* seriously... that everything in the garden is rosy, apart from the brown patches in the lawn of course, and a few thistles here and there—well, every garden has the odd weed, doesn't it?

# Coming out of denial

This is the cornerstone of recovery, and an important stepping-stone to maturity. Someone who has no sense of needing to move on is unlikely to take the often difficult choices necessary for growth. A person who refuses to believe that they have a problem—or *that much* of a problem—is not well placed to begin to address it. In contrast, those who have made the decision to do or live differently in future have already taken an important first step. But note that choosing to do or live differently is a long way from day-dreaming about what a different life might be like, 'If only...'.

## *'I have a problem'*

Coming out of denial will, for a Christian, include being honest with God. If there have been many years of excuses, papering over the cracks and hoping he won't notice, being honest with God can be difficult. I find it helpful to remember that I'm only telling him what he already knows.

If for many years 'churchaholism' has taken the place of spirituality, and grace has been swamped by 'justification by busyness', the notion of drawing close to God can be very frightening. Try telling him how you feel and see what happens. Remember that God demonstrated his love for us by sending Jesus to die for us *knowing* we were sinners (Romans 5:8).

The most difficult part of being honest with God is that we have to be honest with ourselves first—in order to be able to express what we need to express to God. This is the nub of the problem of denial: we'd rather pretend to *ourselves* that everything is fine, that the way we've been living is within normal limits; we'd rather reassure ourselves that anyone who has been raising doubts or voicing criticisms is narrow-minded; we'd rather be congratulating ourselves for being unshackled free-thinkers than saying to ourselves: 'I have a problem...'

The organization Alcoholics Anonymous offers the well-known and well-respected *Twelve Steps* for those who are serious about recovering from alcoholism, but their application can be of much wider relevance. The fourth of the steps is: 'Made a searching and fearless moral inventory of ourselves'. The fifth is: 'Admitted to God, to ourselves, and to another human being the exact nature of our wrongs'. Both these steps are aimed at coming out of denial. They are not easy—in fact, they may feel more like mountain climbing than taking a couple of steps! But if we remember that God is with us, it can give us the courage to go for it.

## Offensive to God

Coming out of denial will include recognizing how offensive it is to God when we settle for keeping up appearances rather than asking for forgiveness and cleansing. Or when we push ourselves harder and harder, using workaholism or codependent helping as an anaesthetic, rather than allowing him to heal the wounds which cause the pain.

If we've been trying to use 'church', or the experience of worship, to meet needs which they were never intended to meet, we have been misappropriating things which God intended for good. If we've been misusing our authority or position in the church, or at home, or at work, and stunting or hurting others in the process, God has seen all.

It's salutary to realize that even the sacrifices we've made along the way may have been offensive to God—if we've sacrificed things he hasn't asked us to lay down. Many Christians have told me of the sacrifices they've made in order to pursue God's call. Some have remained single, some have given up secular employment, or taken jobs which were less well-paid in order to have more time for the Lord's work, and I've had no reason to doubt that they were responding to his leading. But others have told me how they have sacrificed their family life. As a result they've become estranged from their husband or wife and children. I've felt uneasy. Did God really ask them to do that? Or have they sacrificed those aspects of their life which they found easier to abandon than the leadership position or popularity which *should* have been on the altar?

## An exercise in futility

If we're trying to plug a 'black hole' of need with an addiction or a driven lifestyle, we're not only going to cause great offence to

God; we're also going to fail. It's not possible to over-emphasize the importance of this point. *Addiction and drivenness are 'lose-lose' strategies for dealing with pain; there's no 'win' option.* There may be a very short-term positive pay-off that makes it all feel worthwhile and gives us hope that the answer could be in pressing on down that route, but it's a deception.

Paul warned that we shouldn't live like the Gentiles 'in the futility of their thinking. They are darkened in their understanding and separated from the life of God because of the ignorance that is in them due to the hardening of their hearts' (Ephesians 4:17–18). Futile thinking, darkened understanding and separation from God are hallmarks of addiction and drivenness—for Christians as well as for those outside the church. Even hearts which have been given to the Lord rapidly become hardened if they are centred on short-term highs or pain-avoidance strategies. I need to ask myself, and go on asking: who or what is central to my life—as I live it, not as I theorize about it?

In Jeremiah 2:13 the Lord speaks to his people, saying: 'They have forsaken me, the spring of living water, and have dug their own cisterns, broken cisterns that cannot hold water.' Who in their right mind would opt for stale water from leaky cisterns when they could be having the cool, overflowing fresh stuff! Only someone whose futile thinking and darkened understanding were leading them to choose an inadequate substitute instead of the real thing.

## Choosing to stop putting on a good show

Fifty years ago, the preacher and writer A.W. Tozer expressed concerns which must be even more relevant in today's culture. He saw it as one of the consequences of sin that we have become infused with a false sense of shame. He wrote of our need to be relieved of the burdens of pretence and artificiality which incline us to *present* ourselves to the world rather than just be as we are. Tozer assures us: 'Apart from sin we have nothing of which to be ashamed' (A.W. Tozer, *The Pursuit of God*). We should be ashamed of our sin—and move speedily to ask forgiveness so that we can receive the cleansing that's on offer. I say speedily because spending endless time going over and over our sin does no one any good.

It's much easier for God to deal with authentic sinners than fake saints. 'He who conceals his sins does not prosper, but whoever confesses and renounces them finds mercy' (Proverbs 28:13). But we have no reason to be ashamed of our pain, our vulnerability, our inability to sort everything out single-handed, our grief, our weariness, our very humanity. Why is it that we're so severely tempted to opt for putting on a good front when it comes to our sin, trying to minimize it or to justify our actions, yet we hang our head in shame when we're forced to admit to being as human as the next person?

Perhaps it's part of being British... perhaps it's just because we're sinners, but most of us seem to struggle when it comes to admitting vulnerability or asking for help. We'd really rather sort everything out for ourselves, preferably without anyone noticing that we even had a need. As I've said before, it's not a sin to be needy, although we may try to meet our needs in ways which are sinful. Everyone needs help or support from time to time. As children we accepted quite a lot of help, but we probably grew up thinking that part of being an adult is that help is no longer required. As far as most people are concerned, it's OK to accept the help of an expert with a practical repair job, such as renewing a washing-machine motor, but to accept help with more personal matters is seen as a sign of weakness.

## Willing to be human

Several years ago, I was chatting with someone after church. 'Did you have a good Christmas?' she asked. I quickly weighed up the pros and cons of giving a truthful but vague answer, but decided that it was right to be more specific. I replied that I had found the Christmas period very difficult, and went on to explain that it had been our first Christmas without my grandmother, whose birthday was on 23 December. The birthday of my mother, whose death was also relatively recent, was Christmas Day. The person to whom I was speaking seemed to understand how difficult this would have been, and was sympathetic. But it was obvious that it had also thrown her slightly, and she commented that it's easy to forget that counsellors have families too. The same probably applies to church leaders and others in positions of responsibility.

We need to make sure we're not contributing to the myths about certain individuals being superhuman. We must accept our own humanity and that of others, and encourage those around us to do the same. As human beings we do not have limitless time, energy or other resources. We cannot withstand all manner of assault without flinching. When we lose someone we love, we feel bereft; when we are cut, we bleed; pain hurts—even if we're Christians, counsellors, leaders, or all three! We cannot always be all that others might hope or expect—indeed *we should not be* all they expect, if they are expecting more than it is legitimate to expect from another human being.

Being open about the limits to our ability to cope can bring tremendous blessing to others, as well as to us. Margaret, the wife of a vicar in a small market town, was leader of a women's Bible study group. Her daughter, Ruth, was passing through adolescence with even more turbulence than usual, and their relationship was strained. Suddenly things came to a head, and it became obvious that this was more than just a difficult phase: Ruth had serious problems.

The strain was beginning to tell on Margaret, and she decided that she could no longer cope with shouldering the responsibility of leading the Bible study group. In fact, she felt she needed a break from the group altogether—and for a few months rather than a week or two. At the next meeting she was open about her feelings, although taking care to respect Ruth's privacy by not going into details about her daughter's problems. She then went home, leaving the group to continue without her.

Some years later, Margaret told me of the outpouring of love and the expressions of support which she had received, both at that meeting and during her time away from the group. She also told me how the other members of the group had grown during that time. If she had gritted her teeth and carried on carrying on, or just dropped out of sight for a couple of weeks without being honest about how she was feeling, everyone would have been the poorer. Since then, Margaret's openness has encouraged other group members to risk being open about their needs, and within the group there's a very high level of honesty, real mutual support—and considerable spiritual growth.

## Not everyone can cope

If we decide to start being honest with people, we may find that some of them can't cope with it. They may become anxious because their security is in our leadership: our being OK is necessary for them to feel OK. For the same reason, some may find it easier to minimize or dismiss any pain we express: 'Surely it can't be as bad as all that. I'm sure it'll all be better next week.' Others may opt for religious-sounding sticking plasters, such as 'Don't forget we have the victory!' Rather than pausing to hear our pain, and maybe a cry for help, they're reacting defensively to stop our pain evoking pain in them. Perhaps they're alarmed to think how it would sound if they started to 'tell it like it is' too? But we'll probably be pleasantly surprised by how many people are warm and supportive. Some may be released by our openness into a greater depth of relationship—with God as well as with other Christians.

We'll need to be thoughtful and prayerful about what we tell to whom, at what time and in what context. The details of some difficulties (for example: a serious conflict within a relationship) should be shared only in confidence, and only with one or two wise and trusted friends, because in sharing them we are exposing someone else's difficulties too. Some people lack healthy limits to their self-disclosure, and freely share the details of deep and disturbing traumas over coffee after church; this is inappropriate. But it's vital to remember that if others respond negatively it doesn't automatically mean it was wrong to share with those people or at that particular time. Telling the truth about how we feel and the struggles we're engaged in may cause some folk to be upset, but that doesn't mean we're wrong to be open. If they have been finding their security in us and in our being on top of things, it's vital for their long-term well-being as well as ours that they stop—however uncomfortable they may find it in the short-term.

# The truth shall set you free

When Jesus said (John 8:32) 'the truth will set you free', it was to those who knew him, to his disciples. He was speaking about holding to his teaching, about discipleship, and about being set free from the slavery of sin. However, some have been tempted to use this phrase out of context to apply merely to the liberating effect of knowing the truth about themselves.

There is a sense in which 'all truth is God's truth', and many people can testify to the benefit they've received from a greater understanding of the way their lives have been shaped, and the reasons for their difficulties. Much (although not all) that happens in counselling and psychotherapy can be helpful, whether or not this takes place in a Christian context. Likewise, many men and women (but not all) benefit from prayer counselling, finding healing and release as well as understanding. But true freedom in *all its fullness* only comes through Christ himself. Self-knowledge, of itself, is not the answer.

In seeking to know the truth and find freedom, we need to seek the truth in and through a growing relationship with Christ. We need to keep seeking Christ, rather than simply seeking relief from discomfort. If the emphasis is on our comfort, we might bypass some of the painful work which we need to do, under God's guiding hand, along the road to cleansing and healing.

## *Dedicated to truth*

Psychiatrist M. Scott Peck writes of our tendency to avoid truth when it's painful. To make progress, he says, we need to be disciplined and face the pain—being totally dedicated to truth, however much it hurts. He writes:

> ...*we must always hold truth, as best we can determine it, to be more important, more vital to our self-interest, than our comfort. Conversely, we must always consider our personal discomfort relatively unimportant and, indeed, even welcome it in the service of the search for truth. Mental health is an ongoing process of dedication to reality at all costs.*

> M. Scott Peck, *The Road Less Travelled*

The truth is often uncomfortable, but it's the bedrock of the road to health, sanity and life in all its fullness. Half-truths and lies sometimes appear more attractive, less confrontational, even more 'Christian', but this is a deception; only truth brings freedom, and God alone is truth personified.

## Prepared for radical change

We need to be prepared for radical change. It's tempting to tell ourselves that if only we drank, smoked or worked a little less, spent a bit more time with our family, and refrained from saying 'Fine' when people said 'How are you?', all would be well. Sadly, rearranging a few externals is not enough. A bright new window display is of no value if the store-room contains the same old junk. What's required is radical change on the inside. The New Testament calls it *metanoia*, literally a change of mind—repentance.

The truth is that worshipping, serving or being driven by anything or anyone other than God is idolatry. Idolatry is sin. Jesus said (John 8:34): '...everyone who sins is a slave to sin'. Idolatry robs us of all that God's grace would bestow (Jonah 2:8), and God is grieved. Making a few minor adjustments to our lifestyle will not make him see us in a more favourable light. He looks on our hearts, and sees the direction in which they are set.

We may have decided to spend fewer hours working (or ministering to needy people, or keeping fit, or whatever), but if our thoughts are still drifting in that direction at every opportunity, have we really abandoned our idolatry? The only answer is repentance and cleansing. Then we can know forgiveness and a renewed relationship with God. Changes in behaviour can then reinforce a change of heart, but opting for external changes because we lack the will to change on the inside will not work.

## Rooting out the bindweed

Some of us will already have some idea where we need to start. Perhaps a sermon in church has underlined something we've read, and we know that God wants us to take notice. If we're still wondering where to start, re-reading the *Focus points* in this book might give a clue. But don't worry! God knows our hearts, and if they're turned towards him, and we're asking him to speak to us about the next step, we won't have long to wait.

We can pray that God will give us the courage to really listen to what he has been saying to us. We can tell him that we're serious about growing to be the person he intends us to be (if we are serious, that is…) and that we don't want to live any longer with the spiritual equivalent of bindweed—a plant that chokes what it clings to as it grows—restricting our growth and usefulness. Then, as we go about our daily routine, we can take note of the thoughts that come to mind, the promptings we feel in our spirit, and check them out to see if they are from God.

If you don't already keep a journal (a reflective kind of diary), you could consider starting one, noting down any thoughts or promptings each day. I find a journal very helpful, because it's often only as a pattern emerges that I realize that God has been stressing a particular point. If I look back over a month or two's entries and notice that the same issue has come up several times, I have to take it seriously, even if on each occasion it has seemed to be relatively trivial. This applies not just to the 'bindweed' issues, but also to areas of new growth, which may seem insignificant at first, but can prove fruitful if nurtured rather than ignored. For example, my decision to write this book followed numerous minor promptings from a variety of directions over a long period. I eventually took them seriously and concluded that this was what God was encouraging me to do.

We need to be willing to allow God to direct our steps along the road to recovery. For example, we may have decided that our main problem is the pace of our life. However if, after asking God to show us how to deal with this, we suddenly become aware of the none-too-gentle put-downs we keep distributing to colleagues at work, he might be trying to show us that the root of our drivenness is a need to feel significant—a need which we've been trying to meet by putting others down. Yes, the pace of our life *is* too great, but if we focus on trying to slow down we'll be dealing with a symptom of the problem rather than the problem itself.

## Free to be me

Rose became a Christian in the 1970s. Not long after joining a church she bought a Laura Ashley dress, because many of the

Christian women she admired were wearing fabrics with the small flowery motifs which Laura Ashley had brought into fashion. Rose quickly realized that the Laura Ashley-look wasn't for her, and disposed of the dress. It had been part of trying to feel at home in new surroundings, but wearing it had left her with the feeling that she was trying to play a role which didn't fit.

We are to follow Christ, who gives us the name 'Christian'. But following him means more than adopting a mode of dress or a Christianized lifestyle. Discipleship training must amount to more than encouraging newcomers to copy those in the church who seem to be spiritually mature. Our calling from God is likely to be different from theirs, so if we simply rush around trying to do the things they do, getting involved with the concerns which are on *their* hearts, we'll be missing the unique place of service which God has for us, and neglecting to use the spiritual gifts we've received for our intended role.

Jesus said that he had come to bring life in all its fullness (John 10:10), and there is a sense in which the closer we are to Christ the closer we are to being the full human beings God planned for us to be. It has been my experience that as I've allowed him to direct my life I've become more myself, living the life God intended for me rather than being moulded by my reaction to circumstances or the views of others. If two Christians were to allow the Spirit of Christ to fully pervade their lives, such that they were both perfectly conformed to his image (Romans 8:29), would they be identical in every way? Of course not!

## Free to make choices

The church has not always allowed me to be 'me', but one of the delights I've had as my relationship with God has grown and developed has been an increasing awareness of the unique way he made me, and the purposes he has for me. It's a well-worn sermon illustration, but a true one: if you want to know how something was intended to work, you should follow the maker's instructions. The problem is, I have to choose to *act* on my Maker's instructions, rather than playing it safe.

I used to be willing for the church to squeeze me into one of its ready-made moulds. I wanted to belong, but there didn't seem to be a slot for someone like me. It was easier to go with the flow of other people's expectations—easier in the short-term, that is. In the longer-term it was painful, because I struggled to deliver what they wanted, and sometimes failed miserably. And they didn't seem to want what I *could* deliver.

Nowadays I'm well aware of the dangers of going with the flow, but it can still be a temptation to say 'Yes' when I know the answer should be 'No'. But if what comes out of my mouth is 'Yes' when my whole being (including the voice of Christ within) is shouting 'No', I'm not honouring God. The same applies when I know the answer should be 'Yes', but I'm tempted to say 'No'. If I have gone against the truth in order to please someone, or kept silent because I was afraid of the consequences of saying what I believed God wanted me to say, I need to come in confession and repentance and ask for forgiveness. No excuses.

Key characteristics of abusive systems are that individuals do not feel free to think their own thoughts, feel their own feelings and know their own mind, and that God only speaks to a select few. A vital part of healthy living is to recognize my own thoughts and feelings, and to be ready for God to speak to me personally. I'm open to hearing the thoughts and feelings of others, and I know that God often speaks to me through other people rather than directly. But at the end of the day, the freedom to make choices means that I'm the one who is responsible before God for the conclusions I draw and the choices I make.

Men and women who have been physically or emotionally abused will find this particularly difficult. They've been discouraged from drawing healthy boundaries, and their safety may have depended on saying 'Yes' regardless of their own thoughts and feelings. I'm not in any way wanting to minimize the difficulties of leaving behind the effects of abuse, and in no way am I suggesting that an abused person needs to take responsibility for what was done to them when they were much younger and/or powerless to resist. But the truth is the same for all: we need to ask God to give us the wisdom and strength to use our freedom to make healthy choices *today*.

If we know we find this difficult, we can ask for help. But we should take care over deciding whom to ask. Friends can be a great help with some problems, but where the difficulties are long-term and complex, friends may find themselves out of their depth and the friendship may suffer. Under such circumstances it can be more helpful to keep the supportive friends as just that, and to arrange to see a trained counsellor in order to explore the issues in depth.

Sadly, not all Christians who call themselves counsellors are suited to this role or adequately equipped. We have no need to feel awkward about asking for details of someone's accreditation before we begin sharing with them. If, when we've got to know them, we just don't seem to be hitting it off, or they seem to be wanting to run our life for us, we need to feel free to decide to see someone else instead. A good counsellor will expect *us* to do most of the work, but their training and experience should help us along the way, and prevent us spending too much time in blind alleys. In case of difficulty, it's worth writing to the Association of Christian Counsellors (see 'Useful addresses' section at the back of this book). The A.C.C. does not provide counselling and is not a referral agency, but may be able to give details of a contact in your area.

## Abandoning false solutions

The world of the addict is teeming with 'magic' answers. The workaholic hopes that buying a filofax or going on a time-management course will help get things under control. The bottom line is that it's the workaholic's hand that pencils yet another appointment into an over-full day—however sophisticated the diary. A course that teaches people to prioritize their activities more effectively is only a tool; if, a few weeks later, they're still choosing to run a hectic schedule as an anaesthetic for emotional pain, this isn't because the course was a failure—it simply wasn't designed to address that sort of need.

The chain-smoker may try switching brands, or chewing gum between cigarettes; the alcoholic may try a different 'poison', or re-solve not to drink before noon (well, before breakfast at any rate). But such strategies are part of the *problem*, not solutions. Anything which in effect says 'It's not that serious—I only need to...' is a manifestation of denial, not a decision to go for radical change on the inside.

## Not waiting for someone to tell us the answer

No sermon, book, course, counsellor, pastor or other person can present us with a ready-made answer to all our needs and difficulties. An essential part of recovery and moving on to maturity is learning to discern the way ahead for ourselves—yes, with input from others as and when appropriate, but knowing that we ourselves are responsible for the steps we take or choose not to take.

There's a lot to be said for having a trusted friend or two alongside when faced with a difficult or demanding task. But the key word here is 'alongside'—the problem would not be solved by someone marching in and taking over. We need to look for one or two people who will support without taking over. Those who are sure they know all the answers to everything can cause more problems than they solve! We ourselves need to beware of falling into the trap of thinking of our friends as 'the answer'; they aren't! If we look to them to meet needs which God alone can meet, to solve problems whose solutions must begin with us, or to make decisions which must inevitably be a choice of *our* will, the last state will be worse than the first.

## Other forms of help—not 'answers'

Having urged his readers to offer themselves to God (Romans 12:1) Paul goes on (v. 2) to urge them to stop conforming to the world's pattern, and to be transformed by the renewing of their minds. 'Then,' he says, 'you will be able to test and approve what God's will is—his good, pleasing and perfect will.' In another letter, he urges his readers to fill their minds with things that are right, pure and lovely, and to follow the pattern of life they had seen in him (Philippians 4:8–9). 'And the God of peace will be with you,' he says.

If our thinking has been scrambled by an addiction (our own addiction, or that of someone whose lead we've followed) or been narrowed to tunnel vision by drivenness, we need to consider how we can improve our mental diet. Isn't it interesting that at last people seem to have realized that there's some truth in the saying 'You are what you eat', and many have jumped on the healthy-eating bandwagon. But as yet there isn't the same enthusiasm for giving up a mental-junk-food diet of ready-made opinions and 'solutions', and sleazy entertainment, in favour of those things which are right, pure and lovely, and will contribute to our mental health.

I enjoy reading very much, so I've always been happy to use books as part of my mental diet! At the end of this book is a list of suggested further reading for those who would like to do the same. Audiotapes can also be helpful. (If you do not have a local provider, write to Anchor Recordings—see 'Useful addresses' section at the back of this book—for information about their extensive range.)

The studies which follow this chapter may provide a springboard for further thought and prayer. They can be used by individuals or worked through in a study group—although group members will find the studies easier to follow if they read this book first, or chapter by chapter alongside weekly studies.

I've already mentioned journalling. Do give it a try—it may feel strange at first, but this soon wears off. The journalling needs to be honest, though: recording a page or two of pious reflections which might have been written by someone else but certainly not by you would be part of the problem not part of the answer. Honest reflection before God is healthy, and writing it down can help us to clarify what we're thinking and feeling. 'Why did I say yes when I meant no?' can be a helpful question to pursue. 'What might I have been doing or feeling today if I hadn't been so preoccupied with other things?' is another.

## A complete change of scene

For the drug addict or alcoholic, it's very difficult to kick the habit if they're surrounded by familiar places and faces, all of which have strong links with 'the problem'. It's often recommended that they go away for a substantial period of rehabilitation. This makes sense for alcoholics and drug addicts, but not for everyone. I know of a number of church leaders who have felt that a new start was 'the answer', only to find that they'd transported all their problems, lock stock and barrel, into their new ministry.

My husband is fond of quoting some words by Horace, a Latin poet from the first century BC, whose work he had to study at school:

> *Caelum non animum mutant*
> *qui trans mare currunt.*

This may be translated:

> *They change their skies, but not their souls,*
> *They who run across the sea.*

The decision to opt for a complete change of scene needs to be taken only after much careful and prayerful thought. It probably needs to involve others—wise and discerning folk who can be trusted to express any reservations they may have. The sort of questions which need addressing are as follows: what are the key elements of 'the problem' and how many of them will be left behind if I move? Have I already tried moving on and leaving it all behind, and, if so, why didn't it work? Have the options for change within the present situation been fully explored, and, if substantial opportunities for change do exist, why am I reluctant to take them? Is part of my inclination to move and make a new start based on the fact that it would be easier to pull the wool over people's eyes if they didn't know me so well?

## *Accountability*
## *—not shifting responsibility*

It's possible to practise a degree of healthy accountability as part of friendship. Accountability is a tremendous blessing, but it can be quite painful. Ultimately, we're all accountable to God, but he often chooses to use other human beings to good effect. As a counsellor, I'm required, as a condition of my continuing accreditation, to be in supervision. This involves regular sessions in which I have to be willing to give account of myself and my practice. As a member of a church, I'm accountable to the leadership;

if it came to their notice that I'd been behaving unwisely or teaching heretically, I hope they'd not waste too much time before asking me about it.

My counselling supervisor and the church leadership are not responsible for my behaviour—that responsibility lies with me, and with me alone—but they can call me to give account of myself if they see the need. The same applies informally with friends and family members. I have a small number of close friends who regularly ask me how I am—and expect an answer that bears some relationship to reality! I do the same for them. We gently but firmly encourage one another to face how things really are, however painful. Margaret's Bible study group (see page 182) fulfils the same sort of function for her. Under such circumstances, thoughts of uprooting and making a fresh start would need careful testing in case they were the manifestation of a desire to escape from accountability.

# Taking a long-term view

Perhaps you feel 'it's all right for her—having friends like that!' But 'friends like that' are grown—they don't usually arrive ready-made! Margaret's group became much closer and started to grow as individuals because she took the risky first step of being honest with them about her situation and her needs. Trust grows slowly, and there's no guarantee of success, but it's definitely worth a try. You could ask God to show you who might be open to a relationship in which there is mutual accountability. But remember that it will need to develop, and it may take a while before you see any benefits.

Relatively few major problems have instant solutions. Many personal difficulties can only be resolved by a process which involves personal growth, and that inevitably takes time and perseverance. Long-term processes feel much more manageable if they are broken down into small steps.

## *No time like the present*

The truth can only set us free if we choose to allow the truth to impact our lives. And it won't look any more appetizing tomorrow!

A habit of pushing truth aside, shelving it, hoping that it will mellow and ripen into something more palatable, will eventually leave us with an ineffective conscience. James wrote: 'Anyone, then, who knows the good he ought to do and doesn't do it, sins' (James 4:17). So let's not delay—if we already know what the first step on our road to recovery is, let's take it now!

To start with, we'll probably need to concentrate on the short-term, dealing today with whatever God has prompted us to deal with *today*. The discipline of taking today's small step today is necessary because concentrating on grand and worthy long-term plans can be an excellent distraction! Seeing visions of a new way of living and dreaming dreams about how wonderful it will be may encourage us to press on, but they're no substitute for taking today's step today.

For example, if God seems to be prompting us to take more physical exercise, then we can go for a short walk after lunch or tea *today*. We don't need to wait until we can set aside a whole day to go for a hike, or we've saved the money for some new walking boots and a compass! The steps don't necessarily have to be enormous in order to be significant. Choosing to take our lunch into the park on fine days may not sound much of a step, but if it allows us to practise letting go of work (the telephone, the needy people and so on) that could be part of building healthy patterns for the future.

If we've become aware that our lives have become over-focused on religious activities, joining a local photographical or choral society could be a helpful move towards broadening horizons and interacting with a different group. But remember that these aren't answers! Photography and music—and many other worthwhile activities—can be pursued compulsively, so they could be merely a sidestep rather than a step forward if wrongly used.

We need to ask God to keep on shining his light of truth into our hearts and minds so that we don't get seduced by 'answers' that are really part of the continuing problem. We need to ask him to keep us on track. Remember, there's no mass prescription for recovery—ask him what's right for you as your next step. Don't flop into someone else's next step because it's easier.

## Being prepared for the long haul

Yes, take today's step today, but be prepared for a lot of steps! It may be a matter of two steps forward and one step back—but don't berate yourself; just admit to a backward step, be honest about why you took it, and move on again.

We need to resolve to aim for *maturity* and *healthy discipleship* rather than pain relief or tidying up the ragged edges of our lives. We need to encourage others to do the same, to help build a healthier family and community. Churches need to be places in which children and adolescents are able to build healthy self-esteem, based on scripture rather than just on the latest pop psychology, and in which they are shown healthy patterns of relating.

People often say to me that they can't stop their unhealthy patterns of living or working because everyone around them is doing the same, and they can't cope with being 'the only one in step'. If this really is true at your place of work, it might be grounds for deciding to look elsewhere, but not before checking out whether there are others who would be prepared to join you in pressing for change.

Unhealthy patterns in families are more difficult. It's not usually an option to bail out rather than stick with the uncomfortable process of change. Perhaps for an unhealthily-dependent adult child, part of the healing process may be to plan towards greater autonomy. This may include moving out of the parental home, but in any relationship healthy change usually involves working hard to improve communication. I have met couples in which both partners assured me that they'd like to change their family patterns, but their other half wouldn't be willing. Even when family members *are* committed to change it still isn't easy, and everyone has to be prepared to see it as a long-term project. 'Old habits die hard,' as the saying goes.

The same goes for churches. Some are healthier than others. Some see individual growth and health as important for the growth and health of the whole, and some don't. Some are open to change and some aren't. If services and meetings have been taking the place of spirituality, and control has been squashing individual and corporate growth, it may be necessary to leave, but this isn't always the case. It's worth taking time to find out if others are interested in 'doing church' differently (perhaps by using some of the Bible studies at the end of this chapter). If no one else is interested, then it's probably wise to look elsewhere, but avoid rushing headlong into a commitment to a new fellowship and seeing it as 'the answer'.

## Taking responsibility

If we're in a position of leadership, we'll need to own that part of the responsibility which lies at our door. Sometimes leaders feel powerless to initiate change because of what they see as the intransigence of the congregation or the church council. But we're rarely as powerless as we feel we are. *We do have a choice!* If we choose to go on leading a church or a group in a manner or a direction which we believe to be wrong, we have to own that as our choice, whatever blame we may wish to lay at the door of others.

Ultimately, we're responsible to God for how we handle our part of any difficulties; we're not responsible for how others handle theirs. But as Christians we'll want to play our part in promoting good health in the body of Christ. So, as the writer to the Hebrews says: 'Let us hold unswervingly to the hope we profess, for he who promised is faithful. And let us consider how we may spur one another on towards love and good deeds. Let us not give up meeting together, as some are in the habit of doing, but let us encourage one another—and all the more as you see the Day approaching' (Hebrews 10:23–25).

# 'My grace is sufficient for you'

The apostle Paul is seen by many as a hero of the early church, but he had his difficulties, which his critics felt demonstrated a lack of victory in his life. Paul challenged this fiercely, choosing rather to boast of the things which showed his weakness (2 Corinthians 11:30) in order to give God the glory. He makes it clear that he asked God to remove one of his problems, which he refers to as his 'thorn in the flesh', but God did not (2 Corinthians 12:7–8).

Paul would probably have found it easier to have had all difficulties cleared from his path, but the Lord had other ideas and assured him: 'My grace is enough; it's all you need. My strength comes into its own in your weakness' (2 Corinthians 12:9, *The Message*). Paul goes on:

> *Once I heard that, I was glad to let it happen. I quit focusing on the handicap and began appreciating the gift. It was a case of Christ's strength moving in on my weakness. Now I take limitations in stride, and with good cheer, these limitations that cut me down to size—abuse, accidents, opposition, bad breaks. I just let Christ take over! And so the weaker I get, the stronger I become.*

> (2 Corinthians 12:9–10, *The Message*)

## Strength in weakness

It could be tempting to allow giving God the glory through our weaknesses to take the place of moving on in God's strength! If we can approach our weaknesses with Paul's attitude, allowing God's strength to move in on them, they'll become a route to blessing and an even better means of giving God the glory. The road to recovery can feel a bit like rowing against the tide, but if we're prepared to open our tattered sails to the wind of God's Spirit, rather than slogging on with the oars, we may be pleasantly surprised by how much more quickly we progress!

Jesus encourages us to live life his way. 'Walk with me and work with me—watch how I do it. Learn the unforced rhythms of grace' (Matthew 11:29, *The Message*).

So, what are the 'rhythms of grace'? It's a very rich phrase, and I hesitate even at this stage of the book to write directly about it lest by doing so I diminish it, but here goes...

## 'Discovering the rhythms of grace'

Grace brings the elasticity which allows Almighty God to walk in relationship with fallen and fragile human beings. 'Discovering the rhythms of grace' speaks to me of settling into the stride pattern we need in order to stay in step with him, neither lagging behind nor being driven beyond his call.

The picture is of learning to follow the pace and direction of God's steps within an intimate relationship, rather than on working through a list of instructions. The pace he sets for us will take account of our humanity; it may sometimes stretch us, but it will not harm us. It will vary from season to season in our lives, but will never become frenzied—neither will it grind to a halt. The Matthew 11 passage speaks of 'rest', but it's rest yoked to Jesus, going at his pace and in his direction—not the rest of enforced inactivity.

I'm confident that our faithful God will go on working to complete what he has begun in us. May you know the richness of his blessing, and delight daily in all that it means to be a child of the Father, saved, kept, and being made whole by grace.

# Study appendix

These studies may be used by an individual working alone, or by a group. They pick up on subjects touched on in the book, and each is loosely linked with material in the chapter which bears the same number. You can work through from beginning to end, or, if you prefer, begin with the ones which seem to be of greatest relevance to your present concerns.

As you use the studies, pray that God will speak into your situation. Ask him to give you listening ears and a listening heart—and then give him time to respond. Don't rush through a study as if it were a school exercise that has to be completed before you go out to play! Don't feel you have to complete a study at one sitting—coming back several times can be profitable, even if you're not aware of having left it unfinished; you may have had new insights meanwhile.

The studies vary considerably in style. Some involve reading several passages of scripture, or tracing a theme through different parts of the Bible. Others use a variety of methods to encourage reflection, or to stimulate creativity in prayer and worship. Different people will warm to different studies, and to different parts of the same study. If you're working in a group, make sure that you don't just use suggestions which appeal to the group leader! If you're working alone, instead of automatically dismissing those studies which are not in your preferred style, try experimenting with them. You could ask God to surprise you! Alternatively, pick out the scriptures and the themes, and study them using more familiar methods.

# Study 1: Worn out?

Pause and reflect on the hours which have just passed. Do you come to this study after much hectic activity? Are you feeling relaxed or wound up? Pleasantly tired at the end of a busy period, or worn out? (Do you perhaps need sleep more than a Bible study at this particular moment in time?)

Read Matthew 11:28–30, and *The Message* version of these verses which heads chapter 9.

If you have a recording of Handel's *Messiah*, you could listen to the soprano soloist singing 'Come unto him all ye that labour'. (This follows the solo 'He shall feed his flock like a shepherd', based on Isaiah 40:11.) Alternatively, you could sing or reflect upon the old hymn 'I heard the voice of Jesus say' (J.B. Dykes, 1823–76) which takes some of its inspiration from Matthew 11:28-30.

Returning to the passage, note (a) what Jesus says about himself, and (b) what he offers and to whom.

If you are studying in a group, allow a time of silence (at least ten minutes) while you reflect on the three questions which follow. Some people will find it helpful to write down their answers; others will prefer to reflect without writing. If you are studying in a group, you are under no obligation to share your answers with anyone.

1  How does 'coming to him' feel? Familiar? Strange? Risky? Something else?

2  Are there particular burdens you're aware of bringing with you? From what would you dearly love to have a rest?

3  Being yoked to someone means that you have to face in the same direction as them and go at the same pace. Are you aware of following someone else's pace and direction? What might Jesus want to say to you about your present direction and pace of life?

Read Mark 6:30–46. This is the familiar account of Jesus feeding the five thousand, but don't focus on that aspect—concentrate on verses 31 and 45.

Jesus seems to have been concerned that his disciples were being overwhelmed. Have you noticed that Jesus took time out, often to be alone with his Father (for example, verse 46), even though there were still lots of people needing his help?

Read Luke 10:25–42. Notice that after telling someone to 'go and do… ' (v. 37), Jesus makes it clear to Martha that there's also a time to stop doing.

## Further questions

1 Mark reports that 'so many people were coming and going that they did not even have a chance to eat' (Mark 6:31). How do you feel about Jesus' attitude to 'time out' in the Mark and Luke passages? Do you share the same attitude? What about those around you (at home, work, church)? Could you use these passages to explain Jesus' attitude to others?

2 Does your daily routine (or absence of routine) help or hinder you in finding 'a quiet place' or time to sit 'at the Lord's feet'?

## Prayer focus

Take time to pray around the issues raised. If you feel confused or uncertain, tell God how you feel. If you are studying in a group, you may like to share your thoughts with others, but do not feel under pressure if you would prefer not to do so.

You may like to use the following prayer:

*Father, thank you for Jesus' invitation to weary and burdened people, and his offers of rest and time to sit at his feet. I like the sound of 'the unforced rhythms of grace'. I'd like to follow Jesus' direction and pace for my life. Please show me anything that's stopping me doing so. Amen.*

# Study 2:
# What's wrong with religion?

This study brings in many different readings as background. If you are using it in a group, you may prefer to spread it over two or more sessions. Alternatively, people could do the background reading before meeting together.

## Background study

God is holy. In Old Testament times he used outward signs, rituals and commandments to teach his people about himself, and about what it meant to be 'his chosen people'. He drew boundaries for their behaviour; he brought home to them the awesomeness of his holiness, and the seriousness of sin; he taught them how it was possible for sinners to approach a holy God. Unfortunately, they had a tendency to latch on to the signs and rituals; this was easier than being the people God wanted them to be. They also reinterpreted some of the things God said to make them more manageable—something not unknown today!

In Genesis 17:10–11 we read of the covenant of circumcision which God made with Abraham and his descendants. Circumcision was an outward sign of belonging to God's people, and a reminder of his promises to them. But later on, through Moses, God made it clear that the outward sign was not sufficient—their *hearts* needed to be 'circumcised' (Deuteronomy 10:16). What do you think he meant by that?

In the same exhortation, God urged them to take what he said seriously (Deuteronomy 11:18–21). But in later generations these very words were used to justify the use of phylacteries. (God's words were written on pieces of paper, put in little boxes called phylacteries, and tied about the person.) Tiny rolls of paper inscribed with scriptures were also fixed in boxes at strategic points in homes, such as doorways. No doubt this seemed a good way to honour God's word, but he wanted them to *live* it—not box it up and revere it.

Throughout Old Testament times there seems to have been a strong tendency to latch on to that which was visible and elevate its importance, whilst neglecting the inner commitment which was intended to give it meaning. At times, God's people were so drawn to favour the tangible and the visible over the Almighty and Invisible that they slid into idolatry (for example, Exodus 32 and 2 Kings 18:1–4, which refers back to Numbers 21:8–9).

Further examples of the misuse of religious practices:

* Isaiah 1:10–17; 29:13 (words taken up by Jesus in Matthew 15:8–9 and Mark 7:6–7); Isaiah 58:1–9a.

* Hosea 6:6 (quoted by Jesus in Matthew 12:7).

* Amos 5:21–24.

Being from a different time and a different culture it is difficult to appreciate the full impact of the words from Isaiah, Hosea and Amos. The point is *not* that God didn't like the religious activities as such—after all, he did command them! The problem was that the rituals were intended to be *part* of the structure of their relationship with God, but the people had made them the centrepiece, the be-all and end-all.

By Micah's time, it seems that even the priests and prophets had lost their sense of being called by God. Their religious roles were used for financial reward (Micah 3:11) and free lunches (Micah 3:5). Micah scoffed that anyone prepared to prophesy an imminent beer festival would speedily be installed as a prophet (Micah 2:11)!

Enter the Pharisees! They were just the men to knock religion into shape. Unfortunately, they used their expertise to put it beyond the reach of ordinary people. Jesus had a lot of hard things to say about the Pharisees (Matthew 23).

# Main study

Read Matthew 12:1–14. (Jesus quotes Hosea 6:6 in verse 7.)

This passage needs to be read against the backdrop of the passages already read. If you had to put together one or two sentences to explain its significance to someone whose knowledge of Judaism and the Christian faith was limited, what would you say? (This is much more difficult than it sounds!)

Can you explain why the Pharisees reacted so violently (Matthew 12:14)?

Read Romans 2:28–29, in which Paul's words about circumcision seem to capture the essence of what God had been saying in the Old Testament. Also read Galatians 5:1–12, in which the phrase 'alienated from Christ' (verse 4) paints a stark picture. Other versions use different words but the sense is remarkably similar, so there's no escape! Spend time mulling over what these passages are saying.

Then go on to consider:

* How do we cope with (a) God's invisibility and (b) his emphasis on heart-religion? Are we in any danger of being drawn to the tangible and the visible as ways of making God and his commands more manageable?

* How can we ensure that visible signs and symbols (such as the sign of the cross, baptism, bread and wine) are used in ways that honour God?

* Do we/others in leadership ever use religious practices as a way of keeping people (or God?) at a distance? How might they be used positively, for example: to emphasize a sense of community?

# Prayer focus

If God has shown you that you have in any way misused religious activities, come to him in confession and repentance, and receive his forgiveness.

If there are aspects of this study which you have found difficult, tell God about them. Ask him to help you to hear what he wants to say to you about them.

Ask God to enable you more and more to worship him 'in spirit and truth, for they are the kind of worshippers the Father seeks' (John 4:23).

# Study 3: Real sin, real grace, real forgiveness

Read Psalm 32, Hebrews 4:12–16, and 1 John 1:5–10.

David, the writer of Psalm 32, knows what it is to be forgiven. He knows that his unintentional sins, his not-quite-getting-it-right, his breaking of God's law, and even his deliberate wilful rebellion have been wiped away by God—and he's bursting into song to tell everyone how great that is. By the sound of it, he wishes he'd got around to confessing his sins earlier! (See verses 3–4.)

The writer to the Hebrews makes it clear that God knows all. We are not forgiven because he overlooks our sin, or, for that matter, because Jesus sympathizes with us. We can be made clean so that we can enter into God's holy presence simply and only because of the shed blood of Jesus (Hebrews 10:19). Jesus himself did not sin, and as our great High Priest he enables us to approach the throne of grace and receive mercy.

By the time John wrote his first letter (towards the end of the first century AD), the church was no longer in its first flush of youth. John, by then well advanced in years, was concerned about seductive ideas which were leading people away from the truth. There were those who had begun to modify their beliefs to accommodate ideas from contemporary thought—some even saying that they were without sin; 1 John chapter 1 verses 8 and 10 are written specifically to combat this heresy. Others were claiming to be so immensely spiritual that it really didn't matter if they sinned; 1 John chapter 1 verse 6 refutes this sort of error. The reason John mentioned sin wasn't to beat people over the head with how wicked they were: it was to encourage everyone to get on and say sorry to God so that their relationship with him could be restored.

Drawing together thoughts from the three passages, can you make a list of the various consequences of trying to pretend that we haven't sinned? (There will be consequences in three main areas: our personal well-being, our relationship with God, and our fellowship with other Christians.)

Note that the words 'You are my hiding-place; you will protect me from trouble...' (Psalm 32:7) come in the context of having confessed sin and knowing forgiveness. Otherwise, we might be trying to hide *from* God rather than *in* him.

### The full picture

The title of this study is 'Real sin, real grace, real forgiveness'. Some individuals are so painfully conscious of their sin that they find it hard to conceive of God's grace, and lack assurance of forgiveness. How would you encourage someone like this using the scriptures? Could you also encourage them from your own experience?

Others know they're forgiven, and have experienced God's grace, but have become a bit casual about sin. When explaining the gospel to new or not-yet Christians, it's easy to give an incomplete picture; hell-fire preaching is no longer fashionable, but have we gone so far in the other direction that we now fail to explain the seriousness of sin? Have we been tempted to present a message which majors on health and happiness (as do many other contemporary spiritual movements) and leaves out aspects of the gospel which sound less appealing?

Using the references given in this study and in chapter 3 of the book, plus any other scripture references you can think of, make a list of verses and phrases which you can use to develop your thinking about sin, grace and forgiveness along biblical lines.

# Prayer focus

Are sin, grace and forgiveness equally real to you, or do you need to ask God's help in a particular area?

You may like to use this prayer:

*Heavenly Father, thank you that I don't have to try to hide from you even when I know I've done wrong. Thank you that the Bible says that you are faithful and just, and that if I confess my sins you will forgive me and purify me. Please help me to move more*

*readily to confession when I need to do so, and to be more open
to receiving your forgiveness and grace.*

Looking back to Ann Warren's comments in chapter 3 (page 65),
is there a need to pray for greater openness in your relationships
with other Christians whom you know well, or with whom you're
doing this study?

# Study 4:
# Different by design

In a band the instruments are united by a common purpose—and hopefully a common beat! Their different sounds and ranges are a great asset when it comes to weaving harmonies and making music.

It's vital to realize that the New Testament does not paint diversity as an automatic threat to peace, joyful fellowship or even unity. It seems that diversity is to be *expected* in the church, in fact the picture is of the body of Christ being *disabled* without it.

Read 1 Corinthians 12:1–31. Use verses 4–6 as a focal point for exploration:

> *There are different kinds of gifts, but the same Spirit. There are different kinds of service, but the same Lord. There are different kinds of working, but the same God works all of them in all men.*

Note the pattern of *different... same*. Verses 7–11 go on to make it clear that different manifestations of the Spirit's working are given for the common good. Verse 26 explains that the different parts of the body should share some mutual concerns.

Make a list of all the examples you can find in the passage (and from other sources—not just biblical) of this different... same principle in operation.

Do we really believe (by which I mean 'live in such a way as to show we believe') that the differences are part of God's plan, rather than an accident or a mistake? Take time to consider this question. It could be helpful to reflect on it for a week or more. If you are doing this study in a group, consider coming back to it next week.

Are you truly able to celebrate differences (as in chapter 4, page

88)? Is this being worked out in your church or fellowship, or do you think it's possible that people are looking for security in conformity?

If you are using this study in a group, spend time examining your diversity—not just in terms of spiritual gifts but also more generally. The questions can also be used on your own—think of the various groups to which you belong as you work through them.

- Are you aware of different individuals making different types of contribution to the group?

- Do you thank God for other people's gifts, recognizing that they have been given 'for the common good' (1 Corinthians 12:7), or do you feel unsettled by them?

- How do you feel when someone makes a contribution you know you'd be incapable of making?

- Do you imagine that you would have a greater sense of belonging if you were more like those in your group or church whom you admire?

# Prayer focus

If you are able to do so, spend time in thanksgiving for the richness of the diversity of God's people. If in all honesty you feel more unsettled than blessed by the diversity, spend time bringing your feelings to God. Ask him to show you how he sees things.

If you feel under pressure to try to be someone you're not, ask yourself where this pressure is coming from. (From other people? From your inner needs or pain?) Ask God to help you to delight in being his workmanship (Ephesians 2:10), and in being and doing what he intends for you to be and to do.

Ask God to help you to go on becoming the fully functioning part of the body of Christ he intends you to be. (See Ephesians 4:15–16.)

# Study 5: The Lord is worthy to be praised!

This study aims to explore different ways of worshipping God. If you are studying on your own, you might like to come back to it over a period of several weeks, taking up different suggestions at different times. If you are in a group, people may want to follow different suggestions all at the same time! This can be very enriching—agree a time at which you'll come back together to share what God has shown you and the worship you are offering to him. Note: if you are planning a group study, make sure that you have paper, pencils and art materials to hand. It would be helpful to have room for everyone to spread out.

Read Psalm 103, several times, in more than one translation if available.

This Psalm is focused on God—his nature, and his record in dealing with his people. Just reading it through quickly it's possible to miss the richness of the word-pictures used.

The psalm could be read as a catalogue of God's attributes, and dissected to give a multi-faceted picture of the Lord who is to be praised. But is that all there is to it?

> *'Praise the Lord, O my soul;*
> *all my inmost being, praise his holy name.'*

Think of a time when something (for example, witnessing the birth of a child, hearing or playing a piece of music, receiving an unexpected gift of something very precious to the giver) stirred your inmost being. Can you use this memory to imagine how David was feeling when he wrote this psalm?

Choose a few of the following ways of drawing out, mulling over and revelling in the meaning:

- Pick a verse or phrase which made an impact on you as you read it, and read it out loud. If you are in a group, you could share how or why it struck you if you wanted to, but don't feel you have to do so.

- The hymn 'Praise, my soul, the king of heaven' (by H.F. Lyte, 1793–1847) echoes many of the themes of Psalm 103. You could write your own song/hymn/poem/paragraph to sing/read in praise of God, based on the themes from this psalm—and/or on other causes for praise which are very real to you at the moment.

- The truths about God in this psalm are true, whether or not they are part of our personal experience. Some truths we know to be true in a deeper way, because we have seen them in action. Which parts of the psalm can you 'tick' as being part of your experience—right now, or in times past? Which parts are as yet outside your experience?

- You could write a song (or a poem, or a prayer) taking up those parts of Psalm 103 which are outside your present experience, asking God to further reveal himself to you.

- Choose a small part of the psalm and draw or paint aspects of its meaning on a large sheet of paper. (Remember, this is worship, not an art competition.) Themes can be brought out using different colours and shapes—you don't need to confine yourself to a representational picture. The words you have chosen could be incorporated in the picture if you wish, but this is not necessary. For colour work, some people find oil pastels (which blend or rub down to give a variety of effects) easier to use than paints; they are more versatile than felt-tip pens. Experiment! You could try a fabric collage, or create a mosaic effect using fragments of pictures from magazines.

- Are there verses or sections which you could express using gestures, silent drama, dance? (Remember, this is worship, not a performance.) Alternatively, consider reading the whole psalm out loud but using different postures (standing with arms raised, kneeling, bowed in penitence, seated with hands stretched out to receive) for different sections.

Towards the end of the session, reflect briefly on what has happened.

Has unaccustomed physical participation or using your creativity (or witnessing the creativity of others) enriched the worship you have been offering to God?

If emotions have surfaced, have they found a place in your worship, or have they felt like a distraction?

How have you handled any frustrations at being unable to offer 'perfect worship'?

# Prayer focus

Spend a few minutes telling God how you feel, and asking him to help you to grow and develop as a worshipper.

# Study 6:
# Whose lead do we follow?

Write a list (one per line, down the side of a page) of about a dozen public figures who are leaders in a variety of spheres. Now write next to each name some of the characteristics of their particular leadership style. How do you feel about those you have listed—are there any you particularly admire? If so, can you give reasons for your admiration?

Read from the beginning of Matthew 18 to the end of Matthew 23. Jesus' earthly ministry is moving towards its climax, and tension is mounting. There are conflicting ideas about what he ought to be doing. The disciples are beginning to get edgy about where it's all leading—and so are the powerful people, who see Jesus as a threat.

Read the chapters again, and this time make notes on the various encounters Jesus has with individuals/groups. Note what Jesus says and to whom. Also note what others say, and the motives which lie behind their words. (If you are using this study in a group, it might be helpful for group members to make these notes beforehand.)

These chapters do not reveal Jesus to be particularly 'meek and mild'! Jesus was clearly a strong leader who was quite prepared to tackle major issues head-on when the need arose. He stood up to the powerful leaders of his day, and spoke without fear of their disapproval. Yet, when it came to dealing with children, he gave them more time and attention than his disciples saw as proper for a respected teacher. Didn't he realize what all this was doing to his public image as an authoritative teacher and serious leadership contender!

From these chapters (the things Jesus did and said, and the stories he told), draw up a list of the characteristics which Jesus saw as important for those in authority.

As a longer-term project, try reading through a whole gospel and making notes on the way Jesus dealt with groups and individuals. Look at the range of people he was happy to associate with; look at the variety of circumstances under which he met them: in their homes, in the street—perhaps on his way somewhere important, in the temple, out in the fields... What can we learn from such diversity, and more generally from Jesus' style of relating to people?

We live in an age which has no shortage of seminars, books and videos on 'How to get on in life', and 'How to climb the ladder to success'. What assessment might the originators of such material make of the way Jesus went about things?

# Reflection and prayer

Most of us have some sort of leadership responsibility. I don't mean that we all necessarily have an official title of 'Leader of...', but we are in a position to influence others by giving a lead. They may be our own children, younger brothers or sisters, neighbours, colleagues in our place of work, fellow members of our house group, music group, flower-arranging society, parent-teacher association, model railway club... Some of us *will* have official leadership roles and/or titles, but it's important not to undervalue the other areas of life in which our leadership is mainly by example (such as in the home).

Which words would you choose to sum up your leadership style?

Are there aspects of your leadership about which you are uncomfortable? Has the Lord been speaking to you about any particular habits or ways of going about things during this study? If so, do you need to ask the Lord (and anyone else) for forgiveness? (Read 1 John 1:9, and receive the Lord's forgiveness and cleansing.)

Do you think it would be helpful to talk and pray things through with a trusted friend—someone who would help you by walking alongside as you seek to become more like Jesus, rather than someone who would load you down with advice and criticism?

Are there aspects of your local church leadership (or small group leadership) which are causing concern? Don't jump in with both feet! First of all, pray that the Lord will clarify what he has been saying to you, and that he will provide the opportunity you need to talk to the person(s) concerned about it. If it's a major issue, it may be wise to pray it through with one or two other people first, checking out that you haven't misunderstood. Resist the temptation to talk to everyone *but* the people involved; even if you are sharing your concern 'for prayer' it could still come under the heading of gossip.

Consider making a note in your diary to check out your own leadership style at regular intervals, perhaps asking yourself the questions: 'Whose lead am I following?' and 'What are those around me learning by my example?'

# Study 7:
# True compassion

(It would be helpful to have completed Study 4 before using this study.)

Read 2 Corinthians 1:3–4 and Luke 10:25–37.

Paul could so easily have written '...who comforts *me* in all *my* troubles, so that *I* can comfort those in any trouble...'—but he didn't!

People who are driven can feel personally responsible for meeting every need they see. This may include needs which they lack the resources (time, energy, wisdom, skills, gifts, finance) to meet. Yes, we are all called to have compassion, and God has promised to equip those he calls to serve him. Yes, from time to time compassion and our desire to serve the Lord will lead us to take unusual steps, such as those taken by the good Samaritan. But even the good Samaritan allowed the innkeeper to do his part!

Imagine a dialogue between the innkeeper and a codependent Samaritan. (See chapter 7, pages 147–148 for the meaning of the word codependent.) The Samaritan is explaining why he can't possibly leave the inn while the traveller, for whom he now feels responsible, is so poorly. However, he is concerned for others who may be about to be attacked along the same road at this very moment, so would the innkeeper like to borrow his donkey so that he can nip up the road to collect any bruised and bleeding bodies lying by the wayside? (If you are doing this study in a group, you could try some role-play.)

## *Healthy interdependence*

Read Romans 12, especially verses 4–8; also read Ephesians 4:15–16 and 32; Colossians 1:18 and 2:19 in their context.

Which ideas from these passages do you personally find it most difficult to work out in practice? Do you, for example, find yourself threatened by the fact that the parts of the body of Christ are intended to have different functions? Do you envy those you see as closer to the head?

Are you comfortable with the idea of interdependence, or would you prefer to remain independent—a part of the body but disconnected? What are the consequences of being disconnected?

In your Christian community, which of the ideas from these passages do you see being taken seriously? Which do you see being neglected?

Ephesians 4:32 says that we are to be kind and compassionate to one another. This means that everyone has to be on the receiving end too! Do you find it easy to receive kindness and compassion from others?

## Compassion in action

Think of a present-day good Samaritan story which illustrates how several members of the body of Christ could come alongside someone in acute need, showing compassion and offering practical help in different ways.

Then consider how the wider body of Christ might support those doing the helping.

What would be the consequences if someone wanted to do all the helping single-handed? Or if they wanted to be a part of the team of helpers but were unwilling to accept any help or support themselves?

# Prayer focus

Do you want to ask God to help you to be more compassionate? Can you be honest with yourself, and think about the motivation behind this? Is it at least in part because you would like to be *known as* a more compassionate person, or in order to feel better about yourself? If the Holy Spirit shows you that you are operating from sinful or mixed motives, don't despair—ask for forgiveness (read 1 John 1:9). Ask God to go on working to purify your heart, and to give you true compassion. You may find it helpful to reread chapter 7 of this book.

Ask God to show you how to apply the principles of the body of Christ in compassionate action in your family, church and community.

If you find it difficult to *receive* help and are only really comfortable in the role of helper, ask God to help you to begin by receiving more of his love. You could pray that God will help you to trust a few people enough to express your needs to them, and to be vulnerable enough to receive kindness and help from them. If this feels scary, talk to God about it.

# Study 8: Peace

Spend a few minutes reflecting on what the word peace means to you.

- With which other words is it associated in your mind?

- Are there verses or phrases of scripture which come to mind when you think of *peace*? If so, jot them down for later.

- What's the difference between *peace*, and the *rest* which was a theme in Study 1?

People whose lives are dominated by drivenness or addiction sometimes say they'd give 'anything' to find peace, but by 'peace' they may mean 'security' or even 'relief'. (And they don't usually mean 'anything'!) Having tried all sorts of unhealthy ways of finding peace, they have usually found nothing of the kind. Some troubled folk even consider suicide as a way to find the 'peace' they crave.

Many years ago I heard a wise and experienced counsellor say that when people asked her to pray for them to find peace she often asked: 'Peace instead of what?' If you find yourself yearning for peace, can you be more specific about what you mean by 'peace'? And can you answer the question: 'Peace instead of what?' (Peace instead of guilt... fear... anxiety... restlessness...?)

## What is peace?

In the Bible, peace isn't about doing away with problems or avoiding trouble. It has nothing to do with papering over cracks in relationships in order to avoid conflict. Biblical peace is not the same as 'peace and quiet' or 'hush'!

*Shalom*, the Hebrew word for peace, is a thread running through the Old Testament and right up to the present day. (It is still used as a greeting among Jewish people.) Although it can be translated 'peace', its meaning is broader than our English word, and encompasses a sense of well-being and completeness. It has a link with the word *shelem*, which means 'peace offering' or 'fellowship offering' (first mentioned in Exodus 20:24).

In the New Testament the Greek word for peace, *eirene*, is enriched by the Jewish understanding of *shalom*. It is used not only to describe harmonious relationships between people, but also to emphasize the fullness of the restored relationship between God and man, brought about by the blood of Christ which was shed to take away our sin. See Romans 5:1 and Colossians 1:20; in Ephesians 2:14 and surrounding verses we read that the blood of Christ brings Jew and Gentile together, echoing the Old Testament peace (fellowship) offering.

Read Psalm 4. Psalm 4:8 speaks of peace, but I don't think we'd be inclined to describe it as a peaceful psalm! What can this psalm teach us about the biblical view of peace?

Read John 14:27 and 16:33, and enough of the surrounding verses to get a feel for the context. Jesus knew what was about to happen. How can his use of the word peace here enlarge our understanding of its meaning? Perhaps there's a sense of 'peace *in*' rather than just 'peace *instead of*'?

Refer back to any verses you noted down earlier, and, if you can, use a concordance or Bible dictionary to search for other references to peace. Use them to build up a picture of *peace*, and to tease out the various strands of meaning.

# Reflection and prayer

Ask God to show you if you've been on an unhealthy quest for relief (relief from what?) or security. Have you at times used religion, church or other people to meet needs which God never intended them to meet? If you need to do so, ask for forgiveness, and for the Lord to begin to heal the wounds which lie at the root.

Is it possible that at times you have said 'Peace, peace… when there is no peace' (Jeremiah 6:14), even leading others to believe that all is well when nothing could be further from the truth (Jeremiah 23:16–18)?

Are you aware of a need for peace (real peace—not just a truce!)

in any of your relationships? You could ask the Lord to show you the way forward, and how to apply what you've been reading. Do you need to ask for or offer forgiveness?

Are you ready to risk greater intimacy with God? One way to start could be with a meditation on John 20:19–22. (If time is short, you might prefer to do this on another occasion, rather than rushing it—but don't put it off indefinitely!) Read the passage several times, preferably out loud, to get the feel of it. Then sit comfortably, with your eyes closed, and visualize the scene. See Jesus coming into the midst, and hear him saying 'Peace be with you!' Does he want to show you his hands and his side, and breathe on you to impart the Holy Spirit, or does he have something different to say to you, or to do for you? (You could use this meditation every morning or evening for several days, or even longer, as a way of allowing Jesus to show you what is on his heart.)

# Recommended further reading

James Alsdurf and Phyllis Alsdurf, *Battered into submission: the tragedy of wife abuse in the Christian home*, Highland, 1990.

Stephen Arterburn, *Addicted to 'Love'*, Eagle, 1992.

Ann Brown, *Apology to women: Christian images of the female sex*, Inter-Varsity Press, 1991.

Joyce Huggett, *Listening to God* (second edition), Hodder and Stoughton, 1996.

Bill Hybels, *Honest to God? Becoming an Authentic Christian*, Zondervan, 1992.

Anne Long, *Listening*, Daybreak/Darton, Longman and Todd, 1990.

Lawrence Osborn and Andrew Walker (Eds), *Harmful Religion: An Exploration of Religious Abuse*, SPCK, 1997.

David Partington, *Pills, Poppers and Caffeine: Addiction and Your Family*, Hodder and Stoughton 1996. [Out of print December 1997. Copies may still be available.]

Leanne Payne, *Restoring the Christian Soul through Healing Prayer*, Kingsway, 1992.

Peter Rutter, *Sex in the Forbidden Zone*, Aquarian, 1995. [Out of print 1997. Copies may still be available.]

David Seamands, *Healing Grace*, Scripture Press, 1989.

Mark Stibbe, *O Brave New Church: Rescuing the addictive culture*, Darton, Longman and Todd, 1995.

Elaine Storkey, *The Search for Intimacy*, Hodder and Stoughton, 1995.

John White, *Changing on the Inside*, Eagle, 1997.

Dallas Willard, *Spirit of the Disciplines*, Hodder and Stoughton, 1996.

Stephen Wookey, *When a Church Becomes a Cult*, Hodder and Stoughton, 1996.

# Useful addresses

Anchor Recordings, 72 The Street, Kennington, Ashford, Kent TN24 9HS

The Association of Christian Counsellors, 173a Wokingham Road, Reading, Berkshire RG6 1LT